The Story of Parliament

Celebrating 750 years of parliament in Britain

The History of Parliament Trust

THE HISTORY OF
PARLIAMENT
British Political, Social & Local History

Foreword

This year, 2015, marks not only the 800th anniversary of King John's agreement to what became known as the great charter of English liberties—Magna Carta—but also the 750th anniversary of the parliament summoned on the orders of the baronial leader Simon de Montfort in 1265. Though it is no longer seen as the first parliament, Simon de Montfort's remarkable assembly was the prototype for the great institution we know now. The History of Parliament Trust, which has responsibility for a research project creating a comprehensive account of parliamentary politics in England, then Britain, from their origins in the 13th century, is marking the occasion with this book. Its aim is to tell the extraordinary story of parliament's development, and to illustrate how the history of parliament is deeply intertwined with the history of England, Britain and the United Kingdom, and how parliament's work has touched and still touches all aspects of life—society, the economy, culture and belief.

The 19th-century reformer John Bright famously said that Britain was "the mother of parliaments"—that it had exported its way of doing politics by discussion and debate throughout the globe. With this in mind, as well as celebrating parliament's role in the life of our nation, this book sets out its influence in the world, an example as important in spreading the value of representative government as Magna Carta was in spreading the priceless concept of the rule of law.

Lord Cormack, Hon. DLitt., FRHistS, FSA
Chairman of the History of Parliament Trust

ST JAMES'S HOUSE

St James's House, Regal Press Limited,
298 Regents Park Road, London N3 2SZ, UK

www.stjames.org

Typeset in Adobe Caslon Pro.
Printed in the UK by Gavin Martin Colournet on Arctic Volume Ivory.
This paper has been independently certified according to the rules
of the Forest Stewardship Council (FSC).

A catalogue record for this publication is
available from the British Library

ISBN 978–1–906670–36–8

Cover image: *The House of Commons* by Karl-Anton Hickel, c. 1793
© National Portrait Gallery, London

Contributors

Dr Sophie T. Ambler is a research associate on The Magna Carta Project and works on political thought, politics and the church in high medieval England.

Philip Baker is a research fellow at the History of Parliament and a senior research fellow in the Humanities Research Institute, University of Buckingham.

Dr Stephen Ball is a research fellow at the History of Parliament, House of Commons 1832–1868 project, who has written on Irish policing and home rule in the 19th century.

Dr Andrew Barclay is a senior research fellow at the History of Parliament, House of Commons 1640–1660 project. He has written on the early career of Oliver Cromwell.

Dr Paul Cavill is a lecturer in early modern British history at the University of Cambridge and a fellow of Pembroke College.

Dr Linda Clark is the editor of the History of Parliament, House of Commons 1422–1461 project and editor of the journal *The Fifteenth Century*.

Dr Ben Coates is a senior research officer at the History of Parliament, House of Lords 1603–1660 project.

Dr Mark Collins is the archivist and historian for the Parliamentary Estates Directorate and specialises in the architecture and decorative arts of the 19th century.

Dr Robin Eagles is a senior research fellow at the History of Parliament, House of Lords 1660–1832 project. He is the author of *Francophilia in English Society, 1748–1815* (2000).

Dr Stephen Farrell works for House of Commons Hansard. He was formerly a senior research fellow at the History of Parliament.

Dr Stuart Handley is a senior research fellow at the History of Parliament, House of Lords 1660–1832 project and was associate editor of its House of Commons 1690–1715 project.

Simon Healy is a senior research fellow at the History of Parliament, House of Lords 1603–1660 project.

Dr Paul Hunneyball is a senior research fellow at the History of Parliament, House of Lords 1603–1660 project and has also written on 17th-century English social and cultural history.

Dr Hannes Kleineke is a senior research fellow at the History of Parliament, House of Commons 1422–1461 project. He is the author of *Edward IV* (2009).

Dr Vivienne Larminie is a research fellow at the History of Parliament, House of Commons 1640–1660 project and also writes on 17th-century immigration, Huguenots and Anglo-Swiss relations.

Dr Patrick Little is a senior research fellow at the History of Parliament, House of Commons 1640–1660 project.

Dr Charles Littleton is a senior research fellow at the History of Parliament, House of Lords 1660–1832 project. He has also worked on the 17th-century natural philosopher Robert Boyle.

Dr John Maddicott FBA is a fellow of Exeter College Oxford. He is author of *The Origins of the English Parliament 924–1327* (2010).

Dr Henry Miller is lecturer in 19th-century British history, University of Manchester.

Dr Charles Moreton is a senior research fellow at the History of Parliament, House of Commons 1422–1461 project.

Dr James Owen is a research fellow at the History of Parliament, House of Commons 1832–1868 project and author of *Labour and the Caucus* (2014).

Dr Simon Payling is a senior research fellow at the History of Parliament, House of Commons 1422–1461 project and has written on late-medieval landed society.

Dr Kathryn Rix is assistant editor of the History of Parliament, House of Commons 1832–1945 project and a historian of Victorian and Edwardian politics.

Dr Stephen Roberts is editor of the History of Parliament, House of Commons 1640–1660 project.

Dr Philip Salmon is editor of the History of Parliament, House of Commons 1832–1945 project and author of *Electoral Reform at Work* (2002).

Dr David Scott is a senior research fellow at the History of Parliament, House of Commons 1640–1660 project. He is author of *Leviathan: the Rise of Britain as a World Power* (2013).

Dr Paul Seaward is director of the History of Parliament.

Dr Caroline Shenton is author of *The Day Parliament Burned Down* (2012).

Dr Mari Takayanagi is an archivist and historian who works on parliament and women in the early 20th century.

Dr Andrew Thrush is editor of the History of Parliament, House of Lords 1603–1660 project and was editor of *The History of Parliament: the House of Commons 1604–1629* (2010).

Contents

Introduction

There is no date that marks the exact beginning of parliament. Assemblies held by the Anglo-Saxon kings were very different from today's parliament, but there is no doubt that parliament evolved out of them. The parliament of 1265 is remembered because it included representatives not only from each county but also from many towns. It showed that the king and the other great men of the kingdom had recognised that they could no longer make decisions for the whole country without involving a much wider group of people.

Seven hundred and fifty years later, parliament is now a very different body, elected under a properly democratic system. It is still, though, deeply marked by its past, and while democracy has profoundly altered the way it works, parliament's central role—as the body through which the national community considers and agrees laws and taxes—has remained essentially the same.

Parliament is not just about events in London and Westminster—about MPs, ministers and their battles. On the one hand, the essence of parliament is and has always been the presence of local voices bringing their concerns and views to the national government. On the other, the effects of parliament's debates and decisions are and have always been felt across the nation—in laws affecting every area of the nation's life, from its schools to its industries, from its religion to its armed forces, from its shops to its hospitals.

In this book, historians of parliament explain the institution's development over more than a thousand years. They focus on some of the events and people who have been most involved and most influential in it; and they show that while parliament has adapted to changing cultures and a changing population, it has also helped to shape those changes. Parliament's evolution has not been straightforward —sometimes its power has grown, sometimes it has fallen back; its relationships with the government and the people have always been fraught and complicated; it has rarely been exactly popular. Yet its enormous achievement has been to be, over centuries, a forum for the largely peaceful negotiation and resolution of conflict through debate and vote, rather than violence.

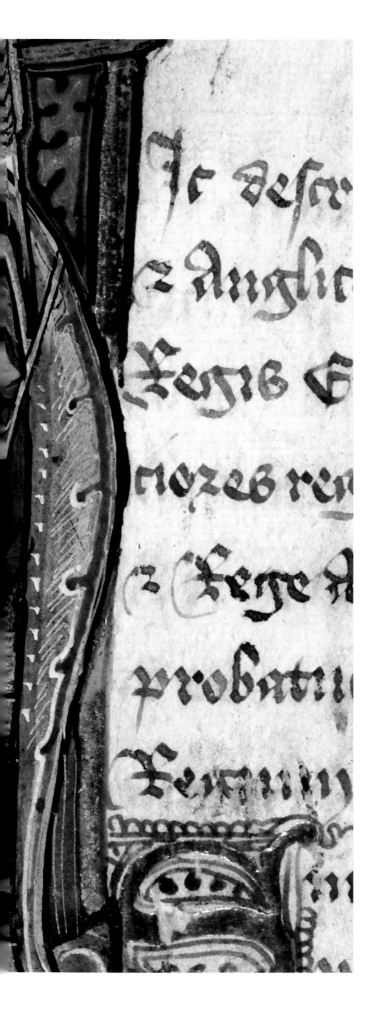

Chapter one—
Medieval origins

The parliament that met 750 years ago
in 1265 was one of the most important
ever. But it was not the first meeting to
be called a parliament. And, long before
they was anything called parliament,
kings were bringing together assemblies
of the most powerful men in the country
to discuss the decisions they had to
make. These assemblies began to change
when kings started to ask not just the great
magnates to attend them, but also people
who could represent local communities.
The king wanted them to agree to
new and ever more burdensome taxes.
The representatives saw a chance to
secure better government from the king.

Contributors—
Sophie Ambler
Linda Clark
Hannes Kleineke
John Maddicott
Charles Moreton
Simon Payling

If we define parliament as an assembly of the country's great men convened by the king to discuss national business, then the institution's origins lie not in the 13th century, when the Latin word *parliamentum* first appears, but in the reign of King Athelstan (924–39). It was then that royal assemblies drawing in nobles and churchmen from most of what was in process of becoming England began to meet regularly.

The background to this momentous development lay in the conquest of the Danish-occupied parts of midland and eastern England by the Anglo-Saxon kings of Wessex, first Edward the Elder and then his son Athelstan. Ruling such a greatly enlarged kingdom, kings could no longer govern it personally, by travelling through their territories; their subjects had to come to them.

The resulting assemblies, often termed meetings of the *witan* or the king's "wise men" by Anglo-Saxons, were on a large scale, sometimes numbering a hundred or more men. They usually met at the great feasts of the church, Christmas, Easter and Whitsun, generally at royal manors in Wessex but latterly in towns such as Oxford and Gloucester. They were concerned with all aspects of the country's government.

During their sessions the king might wear his crown to emphasise that kingship was a mark of superiority derived from God. But despite this display of royal superiority, which also seems to have begun with Athelstan, most of the assembly's work was characterised by consensus.

Throughout the 10th century and into the reign of Cnut (1016–35) law codes were frequently promulgated in assemblies; policy—towards the maintenance of the peace, for example—was discussed; appointments were made to major offices such as bishoprics; and kings granted out lands and privileges by charter. Because they were witnessed by those present at the assembly, these charters made royal patronage more acceptable by indicating general agreement. These meetings were also great social occasions, when eating, drinking and what we would call "networking" forged another bond between the king and his great men. Conviviality was an aspect of consensual government.

The tradition of regular large-scale assemblies established by Athelstan survived through the Danish conquest of England by Cnut and was taken over by another invader, William of Normandy (William the Conqueror, 1066–87), after 1066. The witan was one of several Anglo-Saxon institutions utilised by the Conqueror that contributed powerfully to the Conquest's success.

But this basic continuity was combined with some further developments in assembly practices. William placed a new emphasis on crown-wearing at his assemblies, probably wishing to demonstrate to his nobility the magnitude of his transformation from duke to king. Yet this was a transient change and after the early years of Henry I (1100–35) crown-wearing became much less frequent. More important, and more enduring, were two innovations. Under the Anglo-Norman kings the convention became established that the king's tenants-in-chief—the magnates, bishops and abbots to whom he had granted land—were obliged to attend royal assemblies. Here was the germ of the future house of lords. The obligation of these men was now strictly defined: they were not only to attend, but also to provide the king with "counsel and aid". Aid meant military service, counsel a more pacific sort of support in the form of the good advice which the king expected from his tenants-in-chief.

The counsel sought by the king was a crucial aspect of the assembly's continuing role in promoting consensus. The Anglo-Norman kings were not dictators. Faced with emergencies, they were often undecided about the best course of action—hence the Conqueror sought the counsel of his magnates when faced with a Danish invasion in 1085—and the counsel given in assemblies additionally helped to spread the responsibility for decision-making, for bad decisions as well as good ones.

There were other political circumstances that favoured the continuance of harmony in assemblies. They were rarely, if ever, concerned with taxation. Until the 1180s, the king's income derived predominantly from the "geld", a tax falling largely on the peasantry, from the profits of justice and from

Opposite: King Athelstan presenting The Venerable Bede with a copy of Bede's own Lives of St Cuthbert, a picture from the 10th-century manuscript itself

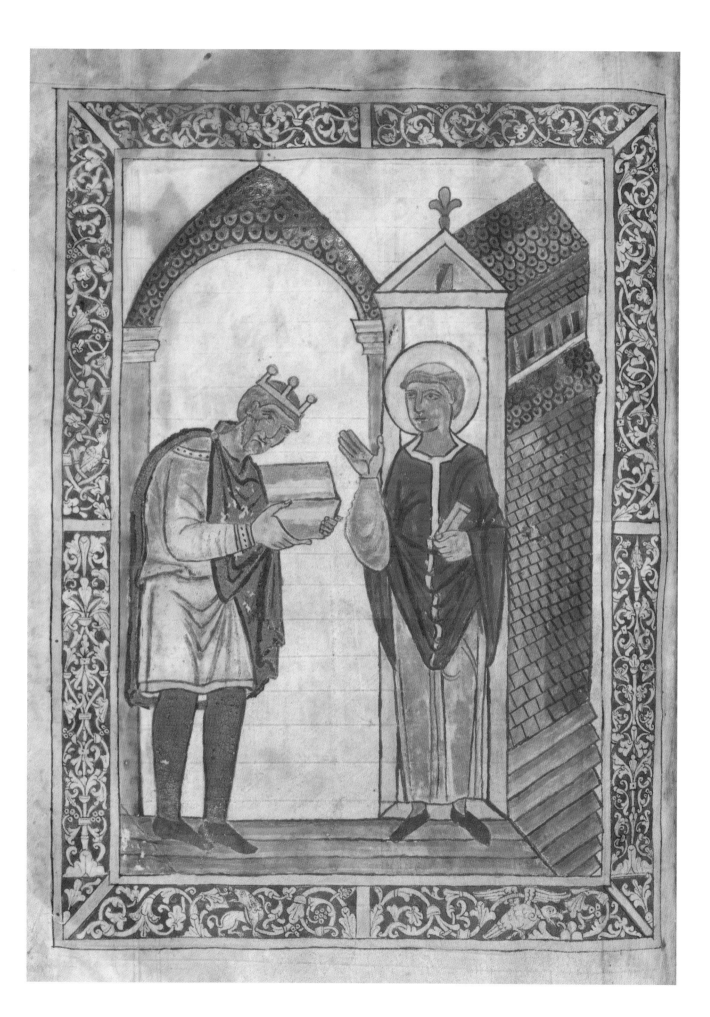

The Lincoln Cathedral copy of Magna Carta, one of the four existing original copies of the charter

Magna Carta

In the 13th century, the original version of Magna Carta was known as "the Charter of Runnymede", after the meadow where it was issued on 15 June 1215. This was a peace treaty, intended to avert civil war between King John (1199–1216) and his barons. Its extensive list of concessions regulated the king's feudal rights, restricted his money-making ventures and set out fundamental principles, namely that the English Church should be free from royal interference, that the king was to govern by law and not by his will, and that he was to provide justice for his subjects.

The Charter also included a controversial "security for peace", which licensed 25 barons to seize the king's lands and possessions if he went back on his promises. Perhaps a dozen or so formal copies of the 1215 Charter were produced, though only four survive today.

The 1215 version of the Charter had a short shelf-life. Within weeks, it was annulled by Pope Innocent III on the grounds that it damaged royal power and had been extracted by force. The new life of the Charter began when one of the most powerful barons, William Marshal, and the Pope's representative, who jointly governed on behalf of John's young son Henry III (1216–72), issued new versions in 1216 and 1217. These versions left out the more controversial clauses but helped to win support for the king during the civil war that had been provoked by John's rejection of the Charter. The definitive version of Magna Carta was issued in 1225, in return for a grant of taxation, and it was this version that was confirmed several times in the 13th century.

Magna Carta and parliament

—— ∫ ——

The early histories of Magna Carta and parliament are inextricably bound. The Charter limited the traditional means by which kings raised money and forced the ruler to turn to taxation (for which he needed his subjects' consent) in order to support his government. Since the Norman Conquest, kings had claimed "feudal incidents". These were lucrative rights that sprang from the king's position as feudal overlord. They could also expect barons to offer payments to receive royal justice.

Richard I had already prodigiously exploited these rights to fund his wars. His brother, King John, intent on raising cash to recapture the Norman lands he had lost to the King of France in 1204, made even greater demands. Laden with debts to a king they could not trust, the barons were forced into rebellion. When King John agreed the Magna Carta settlement with the rebels at Runnymede in 1215, he was forced to concede that feudal incidents would be limited to what was customary and reasonable and that he would "not sell, or deny, or delay right or justice to anyone" (clause 40 of Magna Carta 1215). He also agreed (in clause 12) that he would not levy taxes "except by the common counsel" of his kingdom. Clause 14 of the Charter described how "common counsel" was to be sought.

All of the major tenants-in-chief (bishops, earls and greater barons) were to be summoned individually, while minor tenants-in-chief (those of knightly status) were to be called by a general summons. The practice of summoning lesser landholders to particularly important assemblies was long-standing. King John, however, had levied a huge tax in 1207 without troubling to secure the proper consent of a broad body of his subjects. The 1215 Charter insisted that an assembly representative (according to the thinking of its day) of the wider kingdom was essential to any grant of taxation.

When new versions of Magna Carta were issued in 1216 and 1217 under King John's son, Henry III (1216–72),

clauses 12 and 14 were omitted. Yet those in power remained aware of the practical need to obtain consent to taxation and, in any case, the Charter still forbade or limited other means of raising funds. Moreover, at the very time when the king's options for raising funds had been limited, he was under increasing pressure to find money. Income from crown estates was dwindling because lands had been granted away over the years to royal supporters and because inflation was eroding the real value of what remained. While kings had always been expected to seek the counsel of their greater subjects, now the need to secure support was particularly pressing.

Aware of their increased bargaining power, subjects began to make demands in return. Their main aim was a guarantee that the king would govern lawfully and fairly. They turned to what was now regarded as the standard of good government: Magna Carta. Thus in 1225, in a great assembly at Westminster, the king secured a tax in return for issuing what was to be the definitive version of Magna Carta. Henry again confirmed the Charter, again in return for grants of taxation, in 1237 and 1253.

In 1265, with Henry III held captive, the revolutionary regime headed by Simon de Montfort signalled its intention to govern lawfully by confirming Magna Carta, in a parliament to which elected knights and townsmen were summoned. Montfort's council did not survive the defeat of its leader in August 1265 but Magna Carta, embodying a conservative and cooperative relationship between king and kingdom, endured and was confirmed again under Henry III's son, Edward I, in parliaments of 1297 and 1300.

Opposite: An early 14th-century picture of Henry III enthroned beside Westminster Abbey, the rebuilding of which he initiated, above a family tree showing his children

"From the 1180s, the crown's expenditure rapidly began to outrun its traditional resources"

the king's rights over his tenants-in-chief. None of these revenue sources needed any form of consent, so that consent to taxation, a future cause of contention in parliament, was never an issue.

The traditional characteristics of assemblies, now usually known to the sources as "councils" or "great councils", were maintained in other ways. The making of the law known as the Assize of Northampton at a council meeting there in 1176, for example, showed the maintenance of the assembly's legislative role. Yet one factor increasingly disrupted the old pattern of assemblies. By Henry II's reign (1154–89) the crown's extensive overseas possessions covered most of western France. The king's long absences overseas meant that assemblies, though still frequent, lost much of their former regularity. It was these foreign commitments that ultimately did most to terminate the long history of stable assembly relationships.

The main solvent here was the crown's need for money, as, from the 1180s, its expenditure rapidly began to outrun its traditional resources. Henry II's projected crusade in 1188, Richard I's actual crusade in 1189 and the huge ransom payment exacted by his enemies after his capture in 1192—as well as the continual need to defend foreign territories against an aggressive French monarchy—all created unprecedented financial demands.

To meet those demands a new tax was introduced: the levy on moveables, by which the crown took a proportion of the value of every man's moveable goods. This novel national tax necessitated some form of national consent, best given by the magnate council. When King John (1199–1216) levied a tax of a thirteenth in 1207, in an attempt to finance the recovery of his French lands lost in 1204, he secured the consent of the great council to the levy, but probably only after a good deal of bullying and coercion. The circumstances of the 1207 levy help to explain the new rule introduced by Magna Carta in 1215. Henceforth, said the Charter's 12th clause, no general taxes were to be levied "without common counsel", meaning the consent given by an assembly. Consent to taxation had

arrived on the political scene, and with it a major strand in the development of parliament.

The 13th-century origins of parliamentary politics

The hundred years following Magna Carta saw the emergence of parliament in the form in which it was to retain for the remainder of the middle ages. Evolving from the great councils of the 12th century, it was shaped by the political circumstances of the reign of Henry III (1216–72). Henry came to the throne as a young boy and, with him being a minor until 1227, it meant that the great council's status was enhanced.

The regents who were in charge of the kingdom while the king was a child looked to these periodic assemblies of magnates and churchmen for authority and support. The great council thus consented to taxes, sanctioned the various political acts of the regents, and provided a forum for the three confirmations of Magna Carta in 1216, 1217 and 1225. As a result, when Henry was old enough to take charge himself, it was potentially a much more authoritative body than it had been in the 12th century. Its members had become accustomed to being consulted.

Henry's own aspirations and policies provided the stimulus for the emergence of parliament from out of the council. His chief aim was to regain the Angevin Empire in France, lost under King John and during his own minority. But this was an impossibly expensive ambition. He could only achieve it by securing general taxation but, under the terms of Magna Carta, he could only do this through the great council.

Henry's unpopular domestic policies stood in the way of such grants: he was spendthrift, he was generous to his foreign friends, and his system of justice and government in the countryside—designed to make a profit for the king—was expensive and oppressive. Because of these grievances, as well as their disapproval of Henry's ambitions abroad,

the magnates repeatedly refused to grant taxation. They did so in what we can now call "parliament": a word first used in a political context during the mid-1230s to describe the evolved form of the old great council. Between 1237 and 1258 Henry asked the barons for a national tax on at least 10 occasions. His requests, consistently rejected, provoked parliamentary criticisms of royal policy and responses by the king that may be regarded as the first parliamentary debates.

By the 1240s parliament, assembling generally two or three times a year, had acquired a regular meeting place at Westminster. Several factors underlay this development. After the loss of the crown's continental possessions, the king usually lived in England, staying in the capital. The king had personal interests in Westminster and its abbey, which he rebuilt from the 1240s onwards as a shrine for his favourite saint, Edward the Confessor; and the main offices of government—exchequer, treasury and central courts—were now becoming concentrated there.

Westminster thus provided a new focus for meetings of parliament and, in so doing, promoted its institutional growth. At the same time parliament was expanding to include people from outside the circle of the most powerful magnates or barons. Present in parliaments which met to discuss the king's tax demands were a group who were referred to as "knights". These were members of the country gentry, locally important men. They attended, not yet as representatives of their counties, but as minor tenants-in-chief, the inferior country cousins of the greater tenants who still constituted the parliamentary magnates.

The transformation of these knights into a more representative body was perhaps the most important effect of the next phase in parliament's development. In 1258–59 Henry's persistent misgovernment provoked a radical reaction: the management of the country was taken out of the king's hands and committed to a baronial council of 15, while two far-reaching documents—the Provisions of Oxford and of Westminster—provided for the extensive reform of local and national government in the interests of equity and justice.

But, by 1263, reform had turned into revolution. Civil war broke out and, at the battle of Lewes in May 1264, the baronial leader Simon de Montfort captured the king and his eldest son, the Lord Edward. Seeking to underpin his power with wider support and authority, Montfort summoned elected knights from the counties to two famous parliaments. Four knights from each county were summoned to the parliament of June 1264 and two knights from each county, together with leading men of the towns (known as burgesses), to the parliament of January 1265.

This was not an entirely new experiment, since elected knights from the counties had been summoned to grant a tax to the king in 1254. Montfort summoned them, however, not to agree to taxes, but to join the opposition magnates in discussing the preservation of the new regime. This was a kind of political business from which, so far as we can see, they had previously been excluded.

The Montfortian regime disintegrated after its leader's death at the battle of Evesham in 1265 and the subsequent restoration of Henry III to full power. Montfort's brief rule nevertheless marked a turning point in the history both of representation and of the knightly class. Representation in itself was not a new concept. The Anglo-Saxon witan, sometimes spoken of as "the witan of the English nation", had been seen as representing the country at large, with the king's great men standing in for everyone. But the more direct representation resulting from elections in the counties in 1254, 1264 and 1265, and, in 1265, in the towns as well, gave the localities a voice at Westminster that they had previously lacked. It also helped to promote the emergence of the knights as a political class, with responsibilities both local and central.

These changes, though the product of a rebellion, made an immediate impact on royal government. County knights were prominent in the several parliaments that met between 1268 and 1270 to discuss the financing of the Lord Edward's plans to go on crusade. It was a mark of the political standing that they had acquired during the "reform and rebellion" period that Henry's government had to offer the knights inducements in return for a crusading tax.

In the early years of the reign of Edward I (1272–1307), the crown made fewer demands for money, and as a result, the knights were summoned to parliament infrequently. But, when Edward

Opposite: When the Commons began to meet separately from the magnates in the 14th century, they regularly used the Chapter House of Westminster Abbey, close by the Palace of Westminster

Above: One of the paintings of c. 1400, illustrating scenes from the Bible, that line the walls of the Chapter House in Westminster Abbey

committed his country to large-scale warfare with France and Scotland from 1294 onwards, the elected knights—and to a lesser extent elected burgesses—became fully integrated into the country's parliaments and political system. The agent of change, once again, was taxation, and it was in these years that the crown's need for the consent to taxation of elected representatives as well as of the non-elected magnates finally became established. The late medieval House of Commons was beginning to appear above the political horizon.

Parliament in the late 14th century: the invention of impeachment

Close to the end of the reign of Edward III (1327–77), the "Good Parliament" of 1376 showed—more than any parliament yet—its potential for limiting the power of the crown. For the first time, the Commons elected a spokesman and prosecuted royal officials through the new procedure of impeachment. Highly critical of the government of Edward III's later years, it submitted the longest list of petitions ever sent to a king in a medieval parliament, conducted its own investigations into bad government and demanded the appointment of a new council.

Through its spokesman, Sir Peter de la Mare—recognised as the first Speaker—it voiced its grievances and demands and initiated the impeachment process. The process involved the drawing up of a formal set of allegations against those whom the Commons suspected of incompetence and corruption. It sent the charges to the Lords for them to put the men concerned on trial, the upper House acting as a high court. Those impeached in 1376 were a group of courtiers and businessmen and financiers, including Edward III's chamberlain, William, Lord Latimer, and the Londoner, Richard Lyons.

These events set an important precedent. Although rarely used over the following centuries, the impeachment process enhanced the Commons' involvement in high politics, becoming a means for it

to hold anyone, save the king, responsible to the nation at large. While the crown was often in practice able to block judgements or pardon those impeached, the process would be an important feature of parliamentary history under Edward's successor, Richard II (1377–99). Its use showed up the serious political divisions of Richard's reign, with a series of savage crises ending in his deposition.

During the so-called "Wonderful Parliament" of 1386, Richard's unpopular chancellor, Michael de la Pole, Earl of Suffolk, was impeached and the king threatened with deposition unless he agreed to attend parliament and agree to its demands. Forced to accept handing power over to a council for a year, Richard managed to overturn this arrangement in 1387. Yet events soon

Below: A reconstruction of some of the pictures painted on the walls of St Stephen's Chapel in the Palace of Westminster in the middle of the 14th century. The chapel would later become the House of Commons

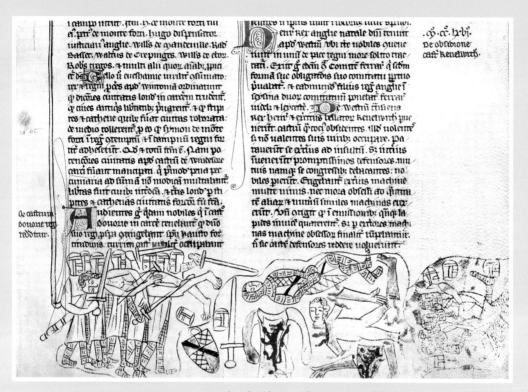

An early 14th-century illustration showing Montfort's fate at the Battle of Evesham

Simon de Montfort and
the parliament of 1265

Simon de Montfort (c. 1208–65) was the first leader of a political movement in English history. The younger son of a French nobleman, Montfort arrived in England in 1230. He persuaded King Henry III to accept his claim to the earldom of Leicester and won the hand in marriage of Henry's sister, Eleanor. But in 1258 Montfort joined a confederation of magnates who, complaining about Henry's unpopular policies, financial mismanagement and corrupt administration, seized the reins of government and established a council to rule in the king's name. As a member of the council Montfort helped to implement the Provisions of Oxford, which aimed to reform central and local government. In 1263 he emerged as the outright leader of the reform movement and, on 14 May 1264, defeated and captured the

king at the Battle of Lewes. Montfort sat at the head of a council that ruled England until the earl and many of his supporters were defeated and butchered at the Battle of Evesham, on 4 August 1265. In an effort to ensure that its rule was generally accepted, the Montfortian regime held a parliament between January and March 1265. Because elected knights and townsmen were summoned to the parliament to discuss the business of the kingdom Montfort has sometimes been acclaimed as a forefather of parliamentary democracy. Montfort was charismatic, pious and possessed of deep convictions, but he was also a ruthless advocate of his own interests, capable of mining the greatest depths of devotion in his supporters and animosity in his adversaries.

*"Although the first known county elections to parliament took place in 1254, it was a long
time before any effort was made to define any electoral process"*

put him back at the mercy of his opponents, led by
the "Lords Appellant". The following parliament,
the "Merciless Parliament" of 1388, attacked his most
prominent courtiers through charges of high treason
and impeachment. The impeachment and execution of
his former tutor, Sir Simon Burley, was a particularly
grievous blow for the king who pleaded in vain for
the knight's life.

When Richard was able to strike back against
his opponents a decade later, he showed little mercy.
The parliament of 1397–98 annulled the acts of
the Merciless Parliament and brought down the
original Lords Appellant, the Duke of Gloucester
and the earls of Arundel and Warwick. But he
subsequently went too far in reasserting his own
power. By banishing two of his greatest lords, the
dukes of Hereford and Norfolk, he set in train his
own downfall. In 1399 Hereford returned from exile
and seized the throne as Henry IV (1399–1413).
Richard was formally deposed on 30 September that
year, at an assembly sitting in Westminster Hall.
Though originally summoned in Richard's name, it
was not technically a parliament since it met a day
after his abdication. Those present reassembled as
Henry's first parliament less than a week later.

Parliament and elections in medieval England
Elections are one of the defining features of
parliaments. Yet they arose as a rather casual
solution to a practical problem. The crown, bound
to seek consent to direct taxation, sought that
consent from the representatives of the political
nation. How should those representatives be chosen?
In the case of those who would come to form
the House of Lords, namely the crown's principal
tenants and the leading clergy, the solution was
obvious: they could simply be summoned by name.

For the local representatives of counties and
towns who would come to form the House of

Commons, such a solution was impractical (although it was,
in the early years of parliamentary history, occasionally tried).
The crown simply could not know who they should most
properly be. A much better solution was to entrust the choice
to the communities themselves.

Thus were parliamentary elections born. We know little
about their early history, perhaps because they were not initially
considered of much importance by either crown or communities.
Although the first known county elections to parliament took place
in 1254, it was a long time before any effort was made to define
any electoral process. All that is known of early county elections is
that they were made in the county court, a regular assembly of local
landholders, and conducted by the crown's chief local official, the
county sheriff. Each constituency elected two representatives, save
London, which elected four. The sheriff would hold the elections
after receiving writs of summons from the crown. The elections
in the towns—usually referred to as boroughs—were subject to a
variety of local customs, differing from place to place. The results
were certified to the crown through the sheriffs.

These early elections (at least in the counties, whose
representatives were the more important group in the early
Commons) were probably dominated by the leading men of the
county court. These would have been the great magnates, usually
not acting in person, but through their own local representatives,
their stewards. Competition for seats may have been so weak
that those returned for both counties and boroughs were often
unwilling nominees rather than candidates. Yet as the crown's
demands for taxation became increasingly frequent the fact
of election began to acquire a new significance.

As the author of the *Modus Tenendi Parliamentum*,
a parliamentary manual written in the 1320s, wrote, "each of
the magnates comes for his own individual self to Parliament"
but the Commons "represent the whole community of
England". So "two knights who come to parliament for the
shire have a greater voice in the granting or denying [of taxation]
than the greatest earl in England". It was this idea that made the
consent of the Commons to taxation indispensable to the crown.
This principle was firmly established in the second quarter of the
14th century. It allowed the Commons to establish a relationship

Above: From the middle ages, indentures like this were made as a record of elections. This one, signed by the sheriff of Dorset, records an election at Lyme Regis in 1610

between their consent to taxation and the king's agreement to deal with their complaints about royal government: in other words, to redress their grievances.

The men attending parliament were now seen as representatives of the nation not just because they came from their communities but because they were elected by them. By the time of the contentious "Good Parliament" of 1376 the Commons had come to place a high value on the right to choose its representatives through election. In that parliament it petitioned the king for a new law to impose penalties on sheriffs who failed to hold proper elections.

Its members had to wait another 30 years before they obtained a statute to govern the process. In 1406 they dealt with the problem that the sheriffs would often manipulate the elections to ensure that one of their own friends or allies was elected. They asked that, in future, the sheriff should return the results to central government not simply by writing the names on the back of the writ of summons that he had received, but by a properly witnessed formal document—an indenture—in the form of an agreement between the sheriff and the electors.

In the Parliament of 1429–30 the Commons turned its attention to another problem. It complained that too many people were attending elections, many of whom did not possess any property and yet claimed an equal voice in the elections as the leading shire gentry. The Commons asked that the franchise be restricted to those with an income of 40 shillings a year from freehold land. Voters also had to be resident in the county in which they voted. In the event of a contest, said the Commons, the candidates who received the greater number of votes should be returned. No mention was made of borough elections, probably because they were considered of less significance than county ones and because the customs of individual boroughs varied so widely.

Nevertheless the statute that was agreed in response to the petition was of great importance. Though it was limited to people who actually owned land, the franchise was surprisingly broad, extending well beyond the ranks of the gentry. It showed that

—in the view of the Commons and the crown—such landowners, as contributors to parliamentary taxation, had a right to be involved in the electoral process. That did not mean they expected them to exercise it very often. The Commons were mainly concerned to exclude from the electoral process the influence of the crown and the magnates, rather than to ensure the rights of the "40 shilling freeholders". Few elections were actually contested.

When they were, it was usually because members of the leading shire gentry had failed to reach a consensus among themselves as to who should be returned. When that happened, it was often because of rivalries within the elite. As a result contested elections were sometimes accompanied by serious local disorder, as happened in Cambridgeshire in 1439 and Suffolk in 1453. Nonetheless, the early 15th-century legislation was so successful that it governed elections for over four centuries. By instituting electoral indentures, it made it easier for the sheriff to resist pressure to make a false return; by defining the franchise, it provided a mechanism for the peaceful resolution of contests.

The turbulent 15th century

Richard II's deposition in the autumn of 1399 marked the beginning of a century of turmoil in English history. From the very outset, the king's supplanter, Henry IV, was challenged by aristocratic rebellions, and his son and heir, Henry V (1413–22), also had to deal with a conspiracy in the early months of his reign.

Parliaments reflected that growing turbulence. In 1399, sanction for King Richard's deposition—by acclamation rather than statute—had been given by an assembly of the estates of the realm, explicitly denied parliamentary status by the usurper. When Henry IV summoned his own parliaments, the Commons in particular began to flex its muscles. It voiced opposition to the crown's requests for taxation, demanded to audit its expenditure, tried to influence whom the king picked to advise him in his council, and mounted other attacks on the indignant monarch's powers. With the crown weakened in prestige and short of money it was at the mercy of a lower House of parliament which controlled the purse strings.

The growing prominence of the Commons was reflected in a heightened interest in becoming a member. Between 1406 and

1446 a series of electoral statutes sought to regulate the inevitable election contests, but the demand for seats meant that elections were sometimes marred by violent disturbances.

With his great victory over the French at Agincourt in 1415, and his triumphant conquest of Normandy (which saw him recognised by the treaty of Troyes in 1420 as heir to the French throne), Henry V restored the prestige of the crown—for a while, at least. For a time, compliant parliaments allowed him to bleed England white through taxation. Yet, when he died unexpectedly in the late summer of 1422, followed just weeks later by the French King Charles VI, whom he had meant to succeed, the dual crowns of England and France were left to an infant. Henry VI (who ruled from 1422–61, and then again in 1470–71) inherited his father's and grandfather's realms at the age of just nine months. He was destined to rule for almost 40 years in total, but his reign was to be a singularly troubled one.

In the first place, the son of Charles VI—the Dauphin, whose right to the French crown had been set aside at Troyes—had not given up his claim to the throne. Much of Henry VI's youth was dominated by English efforts to dislodge Charles from his power base in southern France and to defend their own young ruler's title by force of arms. Once Henry VI was old enough to rule himself, it became obvious that—unlike his martial-minded father and uncles—he had no interest in fighting, and favoured a negotiated peace with the French. In spite of Henry's marriage to a French princess, Margaret of Anjou, his efforts ultimately came to nothing and, in 1450, Normandy had to be surrendered to Charles VII. Gascony followed just three years later.

If the peace policy had been unpopular in England, the ignominious loss of Normandy caused widespread outrage and, in 1450, southern England was shaken by popular uprisings that claimed the lives of several of the king's ministers. The Commons had played its part in the disaster by providing increasingly limited funds for the war effort, but now they turned on the king's ministers and, in 1450, impeached Henry VI's principal adviser, William de la Pole, Duke of Suffolk.

Worse was to follow. The news of the fall of Gascony in the summer of 1453 helped to tip Henry VI into a debilitating mental

Opposite: Some of the earliest meetings of parliament are known to have taken place in the Painted Chamber in the Palace of Westminster, shown here in a picture made in the early 19th century

illness that entirely prevented him from carrying out the duties of his office. It fell to his cousin, Richard, Duke of York, to assume the reins of government as Protector. In the aftermath of the loss of Normandy, York had positioned himself as the principal critic of the conduct of the French wars, and thus in opposition to the court party successively headed by the dukes of Suffolk and Somerset.

The ensuing struggle for power between York and his allies and the court party—increasingly dominated by Henry VI's formidable queen, Margaret—eventually resulted in the open civil wars commonly known as the Wars of the Roses. In 1460 parliament sanctioned a settlement that mirrored the one at Troyes 40 years earlier, in that it disinherited Henry VI's son, the Prince of Wales, in favour of York and his descendants. Queen Margaret was not prepared to see her son deprived of his inheritance without a struggle but, following fresh fighting and York's death in battle, the deal fell apart, Henry VI was deposed, and the duke's son and heir was proclaimed King Edward IV in March 1461.

In the early years of his reign, Edward IV (1461–70, 1471–83) depended heavily on the support of his older and more experienced cousin, Richard Neville, the "Kingmaker" Earl of Warwick, and it was their increasing estrangement as the young king began to develop independent policies that threw the kingdom into renewed turmoil. Warwick orchestrated a series of popular uprisings and, for a time, attempted to rule through King Edward while holding him captive. In 1470 Edward was forced to seek refuge in the Low Countries, and Henry VI was restored to the throne with French aid.

Yet, after a decade of Yorkist rule, the Lancastrian dynasty could call on little lasting support. In the spring of 1471 Edward IV returned and reclaimed the throne. For the next 12 years, he ruled unchallenged, and took his revenge on his French adversaries by leading a major military invasion of the European mainland, the first such expedition since the loss of Gascony. As the reign progressed, the king summoned parliament less and less frequently. Rather than rely on the Commons for grants of taxation, he tried to raise money using a new type of levy, the "benevolence", imposed at the king's behest and relying on the authority of his regal powers—his "royal prerogative"—without the need for parliamentary assent.

It got around parliament's monopoly on authorising taxation because it was, in theory at least, not really a tax, but a voluntary donation to the crown. At the same time, there is no suggestion that the king was actively trying to establish himself as an absolute ruler: parliament's right to control taxation in principle was not in question. And, when Edward went to war against Scotland in the early 1480s, the Lords and Commons were duly reconvened.

Edward IV's unexpected death at the age of just 40 in April 1483 inaugurated a fresh civil war. His young son Edward V was supplanted by his uncle, the Duke of Gloucester, who claimed the throne as Richard III (1483–85). Richard's reign lasted a mere two years before he in turn was displaced by a distant relative of Henry VI's, Henry, Earl of Richmond. Over the course of a reign of 24 years Henry VII (1485–1509) saw off a series of rebellions, most notably an uprising of the men of Cornwall who marched on London in 1497. Like Edward IV, whose eldest daughter he had married, he increasingly sought to rule without parliament, and in 1491 revived his father-in-law's prerogative levy, the benevolence (which had been formally abolished by parliament under Richard III). He was eventually able to pass his throne securely to his son Henry VIII, having left his final parliament in 1504 with the—to the modern mind curious—reassurance that he was disinclined to summon another for a long time without "great and necessary and urgent causes".

Medieval MPs

The House of Commons in the Middle Ages might be said to be more properly representative of the population of England than was to be the case for several centuries afterwards. A medieval parliament contained members with an impressively wide range of occupations and financial resources: from the lowliest rope-maker or baker to the most highly favoured of the king's courtiers; men of small means side-by-side with the wealthiest of the landowning gentry.

Right: King Henry VIII in the royal procession to parliament, 4 February 1512, from a 17th-century copy of the original herald's record of the occasion

To each parliament, 37 English counties sent 74 of the members (less than a third of the house). These "knights of the shire" were often really "belted knights"—meaning that they had won their honours on the field of battle. Veterans of campaigns in France during the Hundred Years' War, bloody confrontations on the borders with Scotland and successful engagements at sea against England's enemies, they included celebrated companions-in-arms of Henry V at Agincourt.

First-hand experience of foreign conquest may have made them responsive to the demands of the crown for increased taxation to fund their country's defence and their monarch's overseas ambitions. Some of these knights would meet their deaths in battle, or by grisly execution after backing the losing side in civil conflicts at home, notably during the Wars of the Roses. One of them, Sir Thomas Blount, was disembowelled, supposedly delivering a defiant speech as his intestines were incinerated before his eyes, while the heretic-traitor Sir John Oldcastle was burnt alive. A few were honoured as Knights of the Garter, with their own stalls in St George's Chapel, Windsor; the epitome of the chivalric ideal, their heraldic accoutrements and code of conduct offered a marked contrast to the gruesome reality of the battlefield.

Most of the shire representatives were substantial landowners, often related to each other by ties of marriage and inheritance. Not infrequently they were kinsmen of barons in the House of Lords, and a minority would later be elevated as barons themselves. Many of them looked to one or other of the great magnates for employment or patronage. "Retainers" may have shared their patrons' interests, yet they did not necessarily owe their seats in parliament to the influence of these powerful men: their own achievements and standing in their localities could be a sufficient recommendation for election.

The Commons would also contain some of the king's leading servants and councillors—for example Richard II's notorious right-hand-men Sir John Bussy,

Opposite: The fabulously wealthy Richard (Dick) Whittington, seen here in a 17th-century engraving with his (possibly mythical) cat, was MP for London in 1416, as well as serving three times as mayor of London

Sir William Bagot and Sir Henry Green (who figure as the villains Bushy, Bagot and Green of Shakespeare's play), and Richard III's henchman the "Cat" (Sir William Catesby)—who were there to do their sovereign's bidding. But by no means all MPs were subservient to the crown. A Speaker like the intrepid Sir Peter de la Mare could courageously express his views, although another, William Stourton, was demoted by his fellows for too-readily agreeing to Henry V's demands before consulting them.

The shire representatives were heavily outnumbered by those of the boroughs—there were two each from selected towns and cities, though London, uniquely, elected four. The smaller towns sent a mixture of lesser tradesmen, inn-keepers, masons, cloth-producers and so on, but the London members belonged to the City's greatest livery companies, such as the Mercers, Grocers and Vintners. They might easily rival and outstrip the knights in terms of wealth, and merchants like the famous Richard Whittington could, through their philanthropic bequests, acquire almost mythical status.

Other major ports such as Bristol, Hull and Southampton elected members experienced in trade with Mediterranean countries, Spain, Gascony, Iceland and the Baltic, while wealthy wool-merchants took on an important role in the business of parliament, not least because of their financial muscle: it was to them that the cash-strapped exchequer looked for loans. There was a thin line between international trade and piracy. The "adventures" at sea of the likes of William Long of Rye, John Hawley (probably the model for Chaucer's "Shipman" in *The Canterbury Tales*), and Robert Wenington of Dartmouth adversely affected the process of diplomatic negotiations between England's ambassadors (who were often themselves members of the Commons at some point in their careers) and their foreign counterparts.

Although a few of the members may have been barely literate, others had attended local grammar schools and a few had been to the newly founded Winchester College. An increasing number had been trained as clerks in the government departments of the chancery and exchequer, where fluency in French and Latin (in which most government and legal documents were written) was essential. The university-educated physician to Henry VI, Master John Somerset, took a seat in the House, as too did the

"Wealthy wool-merchants took on an important role in parliament"

celebrated poet Geoffrey Chaucer. Many studied at the legal training schools, the inns of court in London, and became attorneys or officials in the law-courts based at Westminster Hall. The most able among them rose to be judges, such as the acclaimed chief justice Sir John Fortescue. Yet their tendency to spend more time on their clients' business in the courts than they did in the Commons led Henry IV on one occasion to prohibit the election of professional lawyers to the House.

The author of the poem "Mum and the Sothsegger" complained about the many different ways in which members failed to protect the interests of their constituents—by slumbering through the sessions, taking bribes, gossiping to the king about the doings of the House, or mumbling their speeches incomprehensibly. In fact, medieval members of parliament brought much useful experience to the House—not least of local government, for it was usually the same men who enforced the law in the shires as sheriffs or magistrates, and in urban communities as mayors and bailiffs.

They could be outspoken and opinionated. On one occasion these vociferous, highly spirited individuals had to be kept forcibly in check by Richard II's archers; on another, when told to leave their weapons at home, they arrived in the House armed instead with bats, ready to make a forceful political statement in support of rival magnates. Edward IV found John Hall of Salisbury to be "seditious, hasty, wilful and of full unwitty disposition". It is unlikely that men such as they would seek election merely for the wages their constituencies were expected to pay them. In any case, these, set at the daily rate of four shillings for the knights and two shillings for the burgesses, frequently fell into arrears, and impoverished towns offered seats to anyone willing to accept less, or even a barrel of herring in lieu.

VERA EFFIGIES PRECLAR.^{mi} DOMINI RICHARDI WHITINGTON EQVI. AVRAT.

Huius sparsa viri totū benefacta per vr... ...uensa monstrant indice qualis erat.

The true portraicture of *RICHARD WHITINGTON* thrise Lord Maior
of London a vertuous and godly man full of good Works (and those famous) he builded
the Gate of London called *Newegate.* which before was a miserable doungeon. He builded
Whitington Colledge & made it an Almose house for poore people Also he builded a
greate parte of y̆ hospitall of *S. Bartholomewes* in westsmithfield in London. He also
builded the beautifull Library at y̆ Gray Friers in Londō, called Christes Hospitall:
Also he builded the Guilde Halle Chappell and increased a greate parte of the East
ende of the saied halle, beside many other good workes.

R. Elstrack sculpsit

Chapter two— Reformation

At the beginning of the 16th century, parliaments were already important events, an opportunity for the king to assemble the key people in the country and try to get them to agree to what he wanted (even if he did not always get his way). When they were used to make radical changes to the country's religion, they—and the laws they made—became central to the country's constitution. They also became central to the argument over the most divisive of issues—people's beliefs and religious practices.

Contributors—
Paul Cavill
Ben Coates
Simon Healy
Paul Hunneyball
Andrew Thrush

In 1509, parliament was a significant and respected body. But, as it met infrequently, it was not yet central to the political life of the nation. By 1558, although little had changed in appearance, it had become much more prominent—the principal site for the public conduct of politics. The Reformation was the chief cause of this development. The decision by Henry VIII (1509–47) in the 1530s to reject England's ancient obedience to the Catholic Church under the pope in Rome and to erect a national, royal church in its place enhanced parliament's standing. Parliament increasingly appeared to determine the nation's religious policy.

The Reformation was not a single event, but a process battled over throughout the reigns of Henry's three children, Edward VI (1547–53), Mary I (1553–58) and Elizabeth I (1558–1603). Thirty years of defining, enforcing and reversing religious change confirmed and reinforced the evolution in parliament's function and the growth in its importance.

When Henry VIII came to the throne, parliament was a valued instrument of royal government. As the representative body of the whole realm, it enabled the crown to obtain subjects' consent to new laws and grants of taxation. In theory, the king took counsel on important matters in parliament; in practice, major policies were announced, rather than decided, there. The young Henry was not to be dissuaded from conflict with France from 1512, for example, despite parliamentary fears that a country which had fairly recently emerged from a civil war could ill afford to risk the king's life on the battlefield. MPs and peers did, however, contribute to the making of laws to address social and economic issues, such as hours of work, rates of pay and even the clothes people wore.

Parliament served as a collaboration between the monarch and the political nation, and enabled frank opinions to be respectfully aired. Henry VIII's first parliament in 1510, for example, united around the rejection of the harsh financial policies of the king's father. The early Tudor crown did not need to "pack" parliament—to try to get its own nominees elected in as many places as possible—although it did influence the membership of the Commons. With a large landed estate across the country, it was able to affect the choice of MPs in many places. As seats in parliament became increasingly attractive, they tended to go to richer, better-connected and more important people. A growing number of MPs were royal servants and common lawyers, rather than local residents.

Taxation was still the commonest reason for summoning parliament, because parliament would grant money only for specific purposes—often for wars—rather than on a continuing basis. The value of the taxes granted grew when parliament in 1512–14 (surprisingly agreeing to something that kings had long wanted to do) changed the way taxes were assessed to bring them more in line with the current value of property. Parliament's association with heavy taxation meant that infrequent meetings were probably widely welcomed. A period of peace after 1515 meant that there was no need for more taxes, and no parliament met for the next seven years.

The king's chief minister, Cardinal Wolsey, may also have wished to avoid another parliament after that year's unexpectedly tense one, when a heated confrontation between the House of Commons and the bishops and abbots who sat in the House of Lords had been sparked off by a row about the power of the Church. Wolsey turned to parliament only in 1523, when money was again needed to support the king's objectives in France. The cardinal's bullying manner, although unpopular with MPs, secured large grants of taxation.

In 1525, Wolsey tried to avoid another approach to parliament, with the crown attempting to collect the so-called "Amicable Grant" without parliamentary approval. This provoked widespread protests and had to be abandoned. The incident had reinforced the idea that parliaments were the only way to raise large

Above: Antonis van der Wyngaerde's drawing of Westminster, from his London panorama of 1554. St Stephen's Chapel, by now the home of the House of Commons, is the tall, thin building topped with pinnacles

Opposite: A page from the manuscript of the first Journal of the House of Lords, reporting the proceedings of 21 January 1510

amounts of money. Later parliaments continued to fund Henry VIII's wars, with levels of taxation peaking in the 1540s.

At first, Henry's wish to secure the annulment of his marriage to Catherine of Aragon seemed unlikely to involve parliament. The king's case—that he had transgressed the biblical prohibition on marrying one's brother's widow—was a matter of divine, not human, law. It was the business of canon lawyers in the papal court at Rome and in the universities, not of common lawyers in parliament. The pope's refusal to annul the marriage, however, led to the fall of Cardinal Wolsey and Henry's decision to summon a new parliament.

The Reformation Parliament (1529–36) was intended to put pressure on the Church to agree to Henry's divorce, and not to break with Rome. It passed laws that reflected complaints made in previous parliaments about the behaviour of the Church and its clergy. Taxes paid to Rome were first suspended, and then abolished. Some parliamentarians expressed misgivings, but the king drove the process on.

Having failed to persuade the pope, the crown was forced to assert dominion over the Church in England. The opening move was to bring the English Church's own assembly, convocation, under royal control. The royal supremacy over the Church was publicised in 1533 and formalised the following year. The claim that England was "an empire ... governed by one supreme head and king" was grounded in biblical and historical precedents, but recognition by parliament made it effective.

The break with Rome was a revolution, but it was presented as a restoration of England's ancient freedom. With a consensus in parliament apparently supporting it, opponents were branded as obstinate malcontents, punishable under a new treason law. Nevertheless, opponents emerged outside parliament. Shortly after the Reformation Parliament had ended, a rebellion in northern England, the Pilgrimage of

"The break with Rome was a revolution, but it was presented as a restoration of England's ancient freedom. Opponents were branded as obstinate malcontents"

Grace, claimed that this parliament had been rigged, though in fact later elections would be much more closely managed by the crown.

The origins of the royal supremacy lay in the king's wish to annul his marriage. It was therefore very uncertain whether, freed from Rome, the English Church would adopt the more comprehensive reforms urged by the Protestant movement. The crown took some steps towards reform. Sincerity and greed mingled as motives for the dissolution of the monasteries, which had the side-effect of removing the 29 abbots and priors from the House of Lords.

But Henry VIII rejected most Protestant beliefs. Initially, the doctrinal position of the Henrician Church had been formulated through debate; increasingly, it was imposed by statute. In 1539, parliament passed an act "abolishing diversity in opinions", which created 17 capital crimes. Four years later, it deprived lower-status people of access to the Bible in English.

During the reign of Henry's only son, Edward VI, Protestantism was much more favoured. But it was difficult for a boy-king to push forward the creation of a thoroughly Protestant Church. By signifying the consent of the realm, parliament enabled radical changes to be made, including the abolition of chantries (chapels dedicated to saying prayers for the dead) and the replacement of the Latin mass with an English-language prayer book. The growth in parliament's importance was shown when the lower ranks of the clergy, who had withdrawn from the Commons in the 14th century, sought unsuccessfully to resume their places in order to have a say.

The effect of these changes on the standing of parliament and its statutes was seen when the king died in 1553. His half-sister and successor Mary was hostile to Protestantism and keen to overturn the religious innovations of recent years. However, there was no support for Edward's attempt to block her succession to the throne because that would have contravened the laws made by parliament in the time of Henry VIII. Yet neither did priests dare to resume the Catholic service for fear of the statutory penalties imposed under Edward VI's legislation.

The polarising effect of religious reform appeared in Mary's parliaments. Some members opposed the queen's plans to marry the Catholic Philip of Spain (King Philip II of Spain, 1556–98), delayed the reintroduction of anti-Protestant heresy laws, and obstructed the return to the Church of estates that had been sold off to private landholders. By locking the door to the Commons' chamber and forcing an instant vote, one group in 1555 defeated a bill to confiscate the property of Protestants who had gone into exile when Mary came to the throne. Even so, parliament still approved the re-imposition of Catholicism and the renunciation of the royal supremacy.

A miniature portrait of
Cromwell, painted c. 1532–33,
attributed to Hans Holbein

Thomas Cromwell

As Henry VIII's leading minister in the 1530s, Thomas Cromwell dominated the decade's parliaments. The son of a Putney blacksmith, Cromwell was born around 1485. Returning to England in the 1510s after continental adventures, Cromwell acted as a general legal agent. One of his many clients possibly helped him get elected to parliament in 1523. There he may have delivered a speech urging the conquest of Scotland.

In 1524, the king's minister Cardinal Wolsey recruited Cromwell to oversee the building of his new colleges in Ipswich and Oxford. This experience eased Cromwell's transition to the king's service after the cardinal's fall in 1529. With Henry's favour, Cromwell was again elected to the Commons, where he quickly demonstrated his ability as a royal spokesman. He helped to draft the most important bills in the Reformation Parliament. He then masterminded the nationwide enforcement of the break with Rome.

Cromwell joked how in 1523 he had "endured a parliament" that, after 17 weeks of inconclusive debate, had "left where we began". By contrast, radical decisiveness characterised the parliaments that Cromwell managed, as an MP and, from 1536, as a member of the Lords. By using parliament to confirm the royal supremacy and overhaul government, Cromwell gave it a more important constitutional role. Although early ideas of parliamentary sovereignty may have influenced him, Cromwell was primarily seeking efficient means of advancing his royal master's interests. Cromwell's papers reveal a cultured man of the world, interested in religious and social reform. He may have gone too far for Henry VIII. His reputation as a Protestant sympathiser contributed to his fall from power and his execution in 1540.

Above: The 1534 Act for the Royal Supremacy, which abolished any power exercised by the pope in England

During the period, parliament had swelled in size. Wales had been formally united with England and granted representation in the 1530s. With parliament now so central to English political life, a seat in the Commons seemed a stepping-stone in a public career. As a result, people of higher social status became more determined to obtain a seat. The number of English MPs increased, as boroughs and their patrons sought enfranchisement so that they too could send their own representatives to Westminster. The Venetian ambassador attributed Mary's difficulties in managing the Commons to the gentry, who were proving "more daring and licentious" than the townsmen assembled in previous parliaments. When Elizabeth I succeeded her half-sister on Mary's death in 1558, it was members of the Lords, however, who proved the obstacle to re-imposing a Protestant settlement. Only after the exclusion of several opponents did parliament pass the Acts of Uniformity and Supremacy in 1559.

The parliamentary character of the English Reformation had a strong influence on the Elizabethan Church and state. It emphasised obedience to the law, rather than enthusiastic religious belief. More zealous Protestants regarded themselves as set apart, true believers, often called "puritans". Those who disliked the Protestant changes did the bare minimum they needed to conform to the law. Some held that this "occasional conformity" meant that the Church was being undermined from within by "popery". And now that MPs and peers were accustomed to debate these matters, it became harder to maintain that the crown alone should decide policies relating to the Church. As the 16th century went on, parliament became more assertive in claiming a right to discuss religion.

Elizabeth I and her parliaments

Elizabeth's reign is still often seen as a "Golden Age" of English history. It was an idea first popularised by her own propagandists, and recalled with growing nostalgia after her death.

Parliament was an important part of it. The queen's alleged willingness to enter into dialogue with her parliamentary critics was seen as very different to the attitudes of her Stuart successors. Modern historians partly echo this view. The formal and informal records of debates in the Lords and the Commons—which from this period survive in sufficient quantity to

Right: Queen Elizabeth I presides over the opening of parliament in the House of Lords, in an engraving made in the late 17th century and published in 1682

"For the crown, the main purpose of parliament continued to be taxation. Nearly every Elizabethan parliamentary session voted at least one 'subsidy', the main direct tax"

reconstruct the cut and thrust of debate—show a fractious but workable body. Though parliament would still sit only occasionally (it has been described in this period as "an event, not an institution"), it could act as the fulcrum about which important events turned. Nevertheless, many initiatives ended in failure, and there were some areas of royal policy that members knew well to avoid.

The growth in the size of the Commons continued under Elizabeth. Having grown by 25 per cent under the early Tudors, it increased by another 10 per cent during 1559–86, to a total of 462 MPs. Membership of the Lords, by contrast, stayed roughly the same, at around 80. After the removal of the last of the abbots and priors, 26 bishops were left to represent the clergy. The crown used its powers to give out new titles or peerages—conferring the right to sit in the upper House of Parliament—to 18 laymen. But this was balanced by the 20 peerages that had died out or had been removed from men accused of treason by a process called attainder. Except for important debates, attendance rarely rose above 50 per cent in either House, which left the political initiative in the hands of lawyers, and the crown's servants (councillors, courtiers, bishops and bureaucrats).

Representation was uneven in other senses: the north of England returned significantly fewer MPs to the Commons than the south. London, despite its size, returned only four MPs. While many Londoners found seats elsewhere, they were invariably outnumbered by the representatives of other ports and towns. As the art of lobbying developed apace under the Tudors, this meant that the metropolis struggled to defend itself against rival interests.

The Church was represented by the bishops in the Lords and a handful of Church lawyers in the Commons. They took an increasingly authoritarian stance about Church government, but the puritan clergymen who disagreed with them had their own allies in both Houses. Catholics were marginalised after the Elizabethan religious settlement of 1559 —a handful of Catholic lay peers continued to sit in the Lords, but most Catholic gentry declined to stand for election, although some MPs were sympathetic to their interests. Women were not formally excluded from the political process—some had great influence over individual elections, and a handful are known to have voted—but the only woman with a voice in parliament was the queen herself.

For many members of both Houses of Parliament, the most significant business of any session was legislation relevant to their own social, economic, local and personal interests. Some legislation, such as the Statute of Artificers (1563) or the poor laws (1597, 1601) provided an enduring national framework for social policy. Members were especially concerned about the activities of informers (who made money from discovering illegal activities) and monopolists (people, usually courtiers, who benefited from royal grants of exclusive rights to manufacture certain goods, or to trade in certain markets). Legislation against them was usually stopped by the crown, though Elizabeth occasionally suppressed controversial grants in response to persistent attacks on them. Economic concessions and urban improvements were vigorously promoted by rival towns, while private legislation relating to the land, debts or the legal status of individual people also competed for space on parliament's crowded agenda.

For the crown, the main purpose of parliament continued to be taxation, or "supply". Every Elizabethan parliamentary session apart from that of 1572 voted at least one subsidy, the main direct tax. There were though increasing problems with parliamentary taxation. Evasion became widespread—the yield of a subsidy fell from £136,500 in 1559–60 to £73,500 in 1602–03. The crown's demands for multiple subsidies provoked controversy in the Commons from 1589 onwards. The 1597 Parliament voted three subsidies, but delayed collection for

*Above: A contemporary
drawing of the Trial of
Mary Queen of Scots in the
Great Hall at Fotheringay,
Northamptonshire*

18 months; the resulting shortage of funds contributed to military disaster in Ireland.

Another way of increasing royal revenue was through the customs levies on imported goods. Queen Mary tripled customs rates in 1558, and parliament confirmed these in 1559. There was opposition to this, but it was overcome by referring the issue to the judges. Elizabeth never risked another rate increase, but laid duties on many new commodities. Parliamentary criticism of other revenue-raising schemes often caused trouble for the government.

Among the most difficult issues was religion. The Elizabethan settlement of the Church was resolved by statutes in 1559 and 1563, but many puritans disliked what remained of Roman Catholic ideas and practices. During the 1570s and 1580s, a well-organised group of puritan clergymen and MPs promoted legislation to embed the teaching of the French reformer Jean Calvin within the Church of England, including the replacement of the bishops (appointed by the crown) with a Presbyterian system of elected local synods. Some puritans established an informal Presbyterian system without the approval of the government or the Church, and others lampooned the bishops in print. Radicals formed "conventicles"—religious meetings that took place outside the framework of the Church entirely. Conservatives, including the bishops, secured the passage of legislation in 1593 outlawing these "separatist" groups.

Opposition to the Church settlement came from Roman Catholics as well as puritans, although, after the exclusion from the House of Lords of all but one of Queen Mary's bishops in 1559, they were unable to oppose it in parliament. People who refused to accept the new Protestant ways were the subject of hostile legislation, particularly after Pope Pius V excommunicated Elizabeth in 1570. The subsequent arrival of missionaries aiming to convert England to the revitalised Catholicism established by the Council of Trent (1545–63)

Mary Queen of Scots and the succession

A copy of the formal record of the Trial of Mary Queen of Scots, made for keeping in the parliamentary archives, where it remains

Until the execution of Mary Queen of Scots in 1587 the survival of the Protestant Reformation in England was threatened by the prospect of her accession to the English throne. She was Elizabeth I's nearest relative but also a Catholic. There were other candidates: indeed Henry VIII, empowered by statute to settle the succession by his will, had given preference to the descendants of his younger sister Mary Brandon over those of her elder sibling Margaret, from whom Mary Queen of Scots was descended.

However, the validity of the will was questioned, and the marriage of Catherine Grey, the senior representative of the Brandon line, was declared invalid in 1562, rendering her children illegitimate. Fundamentally, Mary Queen of Scots' supporters claimed that it was not within the power of statute to alter the succession, a view which Elizabeth I seemed to share.

In 1563 and 1566, parliament asked Elizabeth to name an alternative successor, but she refused. In 1572, a bill was passed to debar Mary from the succession, but Elizabeth failed to enact it. In 1584, Elizabeth's chief minister, Lord Burghley, drew up plans for parliament to meet and select the next monarch in the event of Elizabeth's assassination. Implicitly, it would have rendered the monarchy subordinate to parliament, and it, too, was rejected by Elizabeth.

An alternative, and increasingly likely, option was to remove Mary from the scene altogether. In England since her exile from Scotland in 1567, she had been held by the English government under more or less comfortable house arrest due to their worries that she would be the focus of Catholic conspiracies. Her involvement in just such a conspiracy in 1586 provided the opportunity Burghley and others wanted. Mary was sentenced to death under a special act that was passed in 1585, enabling parliament and Elizabeth's advisers to avoid the treacherous constitutional waters of altering the succession or electing a successor. Even so, it required intense pressure to persuade Elizabeth to allow the sentence to be carried out.

Elizabeth officially disapproved of parliament debating foreign policy, except when it suited her. Debate over strategy was reserved for the queen and her advisers. Parliament, though, had to provide the money for campaigns in Scotland and France (1559–62), the battle against the Spanish Armada (1588) and crisis in Ireland (1598–1601). Although ostensibly at peace, she offered considerable support to foreign Protestants fighting against Catholic powers in the first half of her reign, but this was never debated in parliament, because of the diplomatic uproar it would have produced.

The queen was most sensitive about parliamentary attempts to discuss the succession. The circumstances of her birth (Henry VIII had divorced Catherine of Aragon to marry her mother, Anne Boleyn) meant that anyone who upheld the authority of Rome cast doubt upon her legitimacy. Her claim to the throne relied on a parliamentary statute, but this did not persuade her to allow parliament to debate the succession. Several MPs were imprisoned for raising the subject of her marriage; and she snubbed repeated attempts (in and out of parliament) to persuade her to deal with the problem of her heir, Mary, Queen of Scots, who was eventually executed in 1587 for having sanctioned a plot for Elizabeth's assassination. As she was unmarried and childless and over 60 years old, the question of the succession dominated the politics of the 1590s, but Peter Wentworth, who planned to raise the subject in the Commons in 1593, spent the rest of his life in the Tower for daring to do so. Elizabeth only endorsed the succession to the throne of her Stuart cousin, son of Mary Queen of Scots, on her deathbed in 1603.

Parliament and the old Palace of Westminster, 1548–1834

Although the House of Lords met in the Palace of Westminster from the late medieval period, it was only in 1548 that the House of Commons also made its home there. From that point onwards, parliament and the palace were synonymous, though the latter actually had many other functions. The largest structure in this rambling, rather ramshackle complex was Westminster Hall, the principal feature of the medieval palace still surviving today. The cavernous space housed the major law courts of king's bench, common pleas and chancery, as well as hosting coronation banquets, state trials, and makeshift shops selling books and haberdashery.

provoked legislation inflicting house arrest, fines, seizure of estates, imprisonment or death upon lay Catholics, while from 1584 Catholic missionary priests committed an offence punishable by death merely by returning to England. War with Spain from 1585 saw many priests imprisoned, exiled or executed, and mass detentions of lay Catholics. Enforcement of the laws against them, though, was always patchy and inconsistent.

Opposite: William Cecil, Lord Burghley (1520/21–1598), Elizabeth I's most influential and long-serving adviser, painted in the 1560s by an unknown artist. The white stick indicates that Burghley holds a high office in the royal household

Below: *The Palace of Westminster from the Thames, a 1647 engraving by Wenceslaus Hollar, showing The House of Commons in the old St Stephen's Chapel (the "Parliament House"), Westminster Hall and the Abbey behind it*

The buildings around the Hall provided offices for government departments such as the exchequer. To the south lay the former royal apartments, abandoned after a major fire in 1512. It was here that parliament met, the Lords in what had once been the queen's chamber, the Commons in a disused chapel. Meetings of both Houses were generally held in the Painted Chamber, originally the king's inner hall, while other lesser spaces were commandeered as committee rooms. Surprisingly, some peripheral buildings of the Palace were privately owned, a fact which enabled the Gunpowder plotters to rent cellars under the House of Lords in 1605.

These rather makeshift arrangements for housing parliament soon proved inconvenient, as the number of peers and MPs increased and the Lords and Commons began to meet more frequently. Over time the antiquated appearance of the palace also became a source of embarrassment. Grand schemes for a new parliamentary complex were drawn up in the 17th and 18th centuries by the great architects Sir Christopher Wren, Nicholas Hawksmoor, William Kent and Sir John

Soane, but none came to fruition. Not until the early 19th century, when Soane constructed new law courts to replace the old ones in Westminster Hall, was there any significant attempt to bring genuine grandeur to parliament's architectural setting. An impressive royal entrance and larger committee rooms were created at the same time, but the project did not extend to the two Houses themselves.

Edward VI's decision to designate the former St Stephen's chapel as the Commons' meeting place proved a mixed blessing. Originally designed in the 14th century to emulate the famous Sainte-Chappelle in Paris, the building was very tall, but relatively compact in plan. With the antechapel converted into the Members' Lobby, the remaining space became a debating chamber just 33 feet wide and 57½ feet long. Seating was arranged in rows facing inwards, just like the old chapel stalls, with the Speaker's chair and clerk's desk towards the

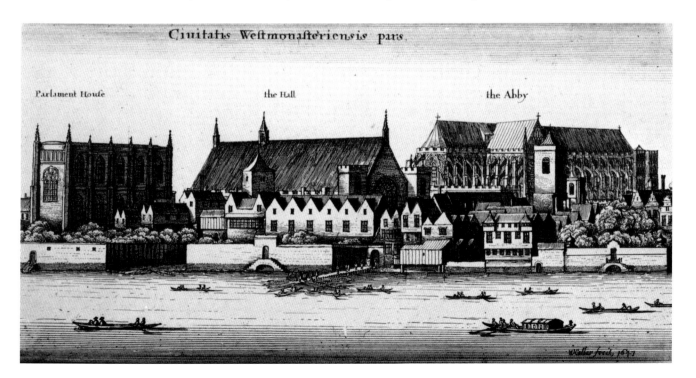

Ciuitatis Westmonasteriensis pars.

Parliament House   the Hall   the Abby

"James's vision of 'Great Britain' was not shared by most of his English subjects"

middle of the room—essentially the layout used for the Commons ever since. The tradition of green upholstery dates from at least the 17th century. From the outset there were too few seats to accommodate all the members.

A gallery was erected at the west end in 1621 but, by the 1690s, more dramatic changes were needed. Wren added further galleries along the south and north walls (doubled in size after the 1707 Act of Union to create space for the new Scottish members), and also transformed the proportions and character of the chamber. The medieval clerestory (containing the upper windows) was removed, sash windows replaced the old gothic ones, a much lower ceiling was introduced, and the walls were lined with wood panelling. The Commons thus assumed the appearance familiar from 18th-century images, and thereafter changed little, apart from the addition of extra seating after the Irish Act of Union in 1800.

Change came even more slowly to the House of Lords. There the arrangement of red-covered benches, with the royal throne at the south end and the Lord Chancellor's woolsack in the centre, was essentially the same as the medieval floor-plan. The chamber was slightly smaller than the Commons. A classical-style coved ceiling was constructed by Inigo Jones in 1623 and, from the mid-17th century, the walls were hung with a famous set of tapestries commemorating the English victory over the Spanish Armada.

As the number of peers increased, seating became a problem, but repeated experiments with galleries proved unsuccessful. A substantial influx of Irish peers after 1800 finally forced the issue, and, as a temporary solution, the Lords moved into a larger room nearby, which had once housed the long defunct Court of Requests. The new chamber, already remodelled in classical taste in George I's reign, proved so satisfactory that further plans for rebuilding were shelved. It was beneath this room that fire broke out in 1834, destroying much of the old Palace of Westminster, and clearing the way for the great Victorian edifice we see today.

Parliament and the early Stuarts

The accession of the Scottish king, James VI, to the English throne in 1603 as James I (1603–25) was warmly welcomed south of the border, largely because civil war had been avoided and the Protestant succession had been secured. James himself saw in his peaceful accession the hand of God, and in his first parliament, in 1604, he declared that England and Scotland should formally unite, for "what God hath conjoined ... let no man separate".

However, even if they were relieved by his succession, James's vision of "Great Britain" was not shared by most of his English subjects, who despised the Scots and feared the extinction of English law and increased competition for land and jobs. As a result, James failed in his objective. Nor were the English pleased when James ended the Elizabethan war with Spain. One result was that several militant Catholics, who had previously looked to Spain for help in opposing the Protestant regime, decided to work on their own. They unsuccessfully attempted, in 1605, to blow up both king and parliament (the Gunpowder Plot).

James was naturally generous and, in the early years of his reign, he lavished land and money on his courtiers, quickly racking up enormous debts. By 1610 matters were so desperate that the Lord Treasurer, Robert Cecil, Earl of Salisbury, offered to surrender a number of unpopular royal revenues if parliament would provide a permanent supplement to the royal income, instead of granting taxes on an ad hoc basis. However, MPs were reluctant to commit themselves and their constituents to permanent taxation, and the "Great Contract", as it was known, was eventually rejected, to the fury of James, who soon afterwards dissolved the parliament.

James felt humiliated by the rejection of the Union and the Great Contract, but his financial difficulties obliged him to summon another parliament in 1614. This assembly proved no

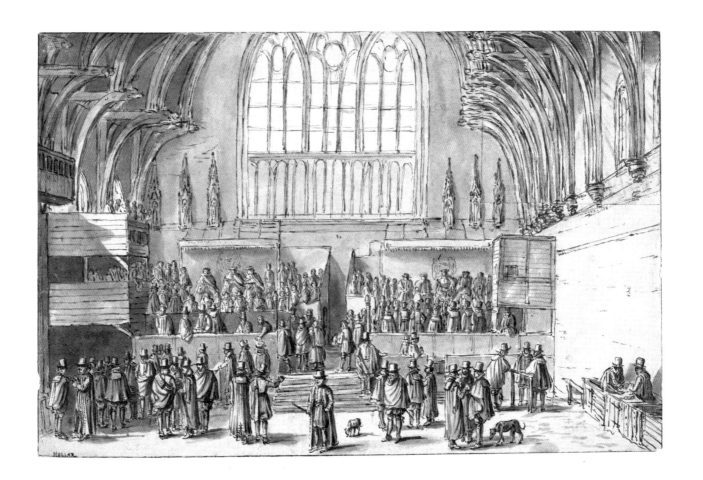

Above: An early 17th-century drawing of the southern end of Westminster Hall. The wooden constructions are the law courts. A staircase at the left led towards the lobby of the House of Commons

were equally determined to prevent the Spanish Match, fearing it would lead to Catholic toleration. James, who still greatly desired a Spanish dowry, refused to allow discussion of his son's marriage. When the Commons protested that they had a right of free speech he angrily dissolved the assembly.

The Commons nevertheless had their way, for in 1624 Charles and the royal favourite, George Villiers, Duke of Buckingham, coerced James into calling another parliament. To popular acclaim, they demanded war and forced James to abandon the marriage negotiations. However, the war, which began in earnest after James's death in 1625 and the accession of his son as Charles I (1625–49), was a disaster. A combined military/naval expedition to Cadiz ended in failure, and English merchant ships soon found themselves at the mercy of Spanish privateers.

Not surprisingly, parliamentary enthusiasm for the war quickly evaporated, and in 1626, far from voting additional money, the Commons attempted to impeach Buckingham, widely blamed for the Navy's failures. Rather than abandon his first minister, Charles dissolved the parliament and raised money instead by means of a Forced Loan (1627). Those who refused to pay were imprisoned and held without trial. However, the Forced Loan was, at best, a temporary solution, for in 1628 Charles was driven by financial necessity to summon another parliament. Charles obtained from it a large money grant, but only at the cost of consenting to the Petition of Right, which declared that imprisonment without trial and unparliamentary taxation were illegal.

The assassination of Buckingham by a disgruntled soldier in August 1628 signalled the end of Charles's military ambitions. Consequently, when parliament reassembled in 1629, the king no longer needed parliament to finance the war. Instead, he wanted it to put the customs duties known as "Tunnage and Poundage", which he had been collecting ever since coming to the throne, on a statutory footing. Many MPs were incensed by this—the king's continued collection of these duties was a flagrant breach of the Petition of Right—but their complaints fell on deaf ears. Charles dissolved parliament, though only after tumultuous scenes in the Commons as the Speaker was held down in his chair by several angry members, one of whom read out a declaration of protest.

more manageable than its predecessor. Instead of granting the king money it demanded the abolition of customs duties laid without parliamentary approval, known as impositions. Since James had summoned parliament to enhance rather than diminish his income, he quickly ordered a second dissolution.

The failure of the "Addled Parliament" (so called because it failed to pass any legislation at all) strengthened James's resolve to do without parliament. Over the next few years he pinned his hopes for financial relief on a large dowry payment for the planned marriage of his son and heir, Prince Charles, to the daughter of the Catholic king of Spain. However, his plans were derailed after the German and largely Protestant territories of his son-in-law, Frederick, Elector Palatine and king of Bohemia, were overrun by Spanish forces.

Under mounting pressure to take up arms to defend his daughter and her husband, James reluctantly summoned another parliament, which met in 1621. Eager for war with Spain, many MPs

Sir Edward Coke and Sir Robert Cotton

Sir Edward Coke (top), an engraving of 1629 after an unknown artist; Sir Robert Cotton (bottom), an engraving after a 1629 painting by Cornelius Johnson

At first sight Sir Edward Coke (1552–1634) and Sir Robert Cotton (1571–1631) represent contrasting aspects of early Stuart parliaments. Coke, first elected to the Commons in 1589, initially enjoyed a meteoric legal career. He held all of the main government legal offices: solicitor general in 1592, Speaker of the Commons the following year and Attorney General in 1594. He rose to become Lord Chief Justice in 1613 but was sacked by James I in 1616 after a series of confrontations with the king. Re-elected to the Commons in the 1620s he dominated the lower House as the champion of the law and the rights of the subject.

In contrast, Cotton held no significant national office. Although he was elected to parliament five times he rarely spoke, possibly suffering from a speech impediment. Nevertheless, at a time when precedents—the records of past decisions—were considered infallible guides to contemporary political problems, Cotton and Coke played a vital role in giving parliamentarians of the early 17th century access to their past. Cotton was the foremost antiquarian scholar of his day who amassed a vast collection of historical manuscripts. From 1622 it was housed within the precincts of Westminster Palace, easily accessible to MPs.

One of those who made use of Cotton's library was Coke, who also accumulated his own large collection of books and manuscripts. The precedents that this antiquarian learning provided played a vital role in most of the major constitutional developments in parliament in the 1620s, in particular the revival of the medieval practice of impeachment in 1621 and formulating the Petition of Right in 1628, with Coke playing a pivotal role in both developments.

Above: Sir John Finch, Baron Finch (1584–1660), Speaker of the House of Commons in 1628–29, who at the end of the session was forcibly prevented from adjourning the House while it recorded its complaints against the government

Opposite: This 1624 engraving is the first known picture of the interior of the chamber of the House of Commons

Like his father before him, Charles now decided to rule without parliament. On the face of it, the "Personal Rule", which lasted 11 years, was astonishingly successful. Charles doubled his ordinary income, for with peace came prosperity and a dramatic increase in customs receipts. He also discovered a way to put a large fleet to sea every year without the need to summon parliament. This involved demanding the payment of "Ship Money", a medieval levy raised in time of national emergency. Ship Money brought in a lot of revenue, because those responsible for its collection were held personally liable for any money not collected. However, Ship Money was immensely unpopular and of doubtful legality: when the Buckinghamshire gentleman John Hampden was prosecuted after he refused to pay in 1637, he was supported by five of the 12 judges.

No less unpopular than Ship Money were changes to the Church. During the 1620s a number of clerics—known collectively as Arminians, after the Dutch theologian Jacob Arminius—were seen as threatening the reformed character of the Church of England. Their most prominent spokesman was William Laud, who became archbishop of Canterbury in 1633. Laud believed that the English Church had veered too far from its medieval, Catholic past and he reinstituted ceremonies and practices that, to his critics, looked very much like Roman Catholicism. Laud was encouraged by the king, who restored diplomatic relations with Rome, and in 1637 the two men attempted to impose a new, English-style prayer book on the Scots. The Scots suspected that Laud was trying to reintroduce Catholicism by the back door. Many of the Scottish nobility, gentry, and leading townsmen signed a pledge, called the National Covenant, to resist the changes. Before long Scotland was in open rebellion.

Following an initial, unsuccessful attempt to crush the Covenanters (as the rebels were known), Charles—needing funds to resume the war—was forced to allow a parliament to meet in the spring of 1640. However, there was widespread sympathy for the Scots in parliament. Indeed some members, like John Pym, were in close, and treasonable, touch with the Covenanters, whose victory they desired. Pym claimed that the Scottish war was evidence of the existence of a wider plot "to reduce our land to the Pope". This plot included not only the promotion of Arminians and the 11-year absence of parliament but also Ship Money and the continued collection of Tunnage and Poundage. It soon became clear that the Commons were more interested in debating their grievances than voting taxes for the war. Not surprisingly, after just three weeks Charles lost patience and brought down the curtain on the "Short Parliament".

Chapter three— Revolutions

By the early 1600s, parliaments had become so prominent a part of the constitution that confrontations between the king and leading politicians would inevitably be fought out in them. In the 1640s, these confrontations would descend into real violence, civil war and revolution. And, although the old order was eventually restored, another, less violent, revolution 40 years later would have a profound effect on England's government, politics and even its religion.

Contributors—
Philip Baker
Andrew Barclay
Vivienne Larminie
Patrick Little
Stephen Roberts
David Scott
Paul Seaward

Previous pages: A detail from a print by Wencelaus Hollar showing the trial of Thomas Wentworth, Earl of Strafford, in Westminster Hall in 1641. The prosecution of Strafford was an attack on many aspects of the government of Charles I

Opposite: A print by Hollar showing incidents that helped to lead to civil war—(top) Pym reports to the Commons on a plot to assassinate him, and (bottom) one of the king's officers attacks a pro-parliamentary demonstration

Denied parliamentary support, Charles's second attempt to crush the Covenanters by force would end disastrously. Undermined by taxpayers' strikes and what amounted to a coup by leading English puritans, royal government virtually collapsed during the summer of 1640. With a Scottish army occupying Northumberland by September, and his treasury empty, the king was forced to call another parliament to meet the costs of defeat. A majority of members in this so-called "Long Parliament" (it would sit until 1653) supported the abolition of ship money and other "unparliamentary" taxes and demanded that the Church be purged of the changes that had been introduced in the 1630s under Archbishop Laud.

But the parliamentary leadership, known as "the junto", had a more divisive agenda. Having treasonously conspired against the king, Pym and his confederates could ensure that he did not exact revenge only by levering themselves into government and destroying Charles's prerogative power. This strategy could only succeed with the backing of the junto's Scottish Covenanter allies; and the price of their support was further religious reform, notably the introduction of a Presbyterian system of Church government, which many in England found insufferable.

The puritan-Covenanter ascendancy in Britain helped to provoke a mass uprising in Ireland, where most of the country remained strongly Catholic. Much of Ireland was soon liberated from English control. Yet far from uniting Charles and the junto against the Irish insurgents, the uprising put them on collision course, for neither side would trust the other with an army. Moreover, many puritans saw the Irish uprising as proof of the claim that there was a "popish plot" against Protestantism that involved the king's court. When parliament began raising forces for Ireland, the king responded in January 1642 by taking an armed retinue to Westminster in a bungled attempt to arrest five members of the junto.

This assault on parliament lost Charles so much support that he had to flee London. But the junto's own assault on the established order had gone too far to leave him permanently friendless. Royal propaganda successfully re-branded Charles as a law-abiding Protestant monarch and the junto as puritan demagogues. By July 1642, Charles was joined at York by many lords and gentlemen (including MPs) who were prepared to fight in defence of monarchy and the Church of England. They left a parliament that was dominated by the junto.

Parliament and the king raised armies in the summer of 1642, convinced that one battle would decide the issue. But when they met at Edgehill, in October, the result was a bloody draw. Faced with a protracted civil war, the junto split into war and peace parties—small groups of parliamentary "grandees" that vied for support among the less committed majority. Royalist victories during the first year of the war encouraged the peace party to seek a negotiated settlement. But the war party exploited evidence of Catholic support for Charles in all three kingdoms to push for a military alliance with the Covenanters and for total victory.

In September 1643, Westminster and Edinburgh ratified the Solemn League and Covenant by which the Scots agreed to help parliament defeat the king in return for (vague) pledges to extend Presbyterianism to England and Ireland. In order to fund and manage the war effort, parliament began to introduce new forms of taxation and to create a powerful executive and bureaucracy centred upon permanent committees with members of both Houses.

The large Covenanter army that marched into England early in 1644 helped to secure parliamentarian victory at Marston Moor in July, and to wrest northern England from royalist control. But it was unable to strike decisively southwards in case it was needed in Scotland. There, an army of Gaelic clansmen under James, Marquess of

a Letter sent to Mr Prm,

Mr Prm, doe not think that a guard of men can protect you, if you persist in your traiterous Courses and wiked designes, I haue sent a Paper=messenger to you, and if this does not touch your heart, a dag= ger shall, so soon as I am recouered of my plague= =sore: In the meane time you may be forborn, because no better man may be endan= gered for you

Repent, Traitor

Colonell Lunsford assaulting the Londoners at Westminster Hall, with a great rout of ruffinly Cavaleires

"The execution of Charles I did nothing to resolve the questions that were raised by the civil war"

Montrose, came close to toppling the Covenanter regime in 1645 and marching to the king's assistance in England. The war party grandees instead turned to the best of their English commanders —notably Oliver Cromwell—many of whom had more radical religious convictions, wanting individual congregations to be independent of any national church. Deserted by their war-party allies, the leaders of the Scots joined forces with the peace party to resist the spread of such radical ideas in England.

As a result of this shift in alliances the war party and peace party grandees acquired new labels: the Independents and the Presbyterians. Further parliamentarian defeats in 1644 gave the Independents a majority at Westminster that winter for merging parliament's armies into a single, properly funded force—the New Model Army—and for replacing peace-minded commanders with Cromwell and other officers determined to fight for absolute victory. The New Model under Sir Thomas Fairfax defeated the king decisively at Naseby in June 1645. By mid-1646 it had mopped up royalist resistance across England.

Defeated, with his peace overtures rejected by the Independents—the dominant party at Westminster—Charles fled in May 1646 to the Scottish army, still based in northern England. The Scots were now prepared to restore Charles to his throne, if necessary by force, but only if he accepted a Presbyterian religious settlement. But the king refused to agree to a solution that required him to renounce government of the Church by bishops. The Scots, unwilling to defy the New Model for a king who did not support their aims, gave him up to parliament early in 1647, and marched home.

By 1647, widespread longing for a return to the traditional political and religious order had tilted the balance of power at Westminster towards the Presbyterians. They wanted to dismantle the massive parliamentary state created since 1642 and to suppress the radical movements that had grown up during the war, particularly in London. But their determination to disband the New Model on the cheap so angered the army that it defied parliament, seized the king, and, in August, took control of London.

The army, allied with the Independent grandees, offered generous peace terms to Charles. But the king, angling for an even better deal, secretly signed the "Engagement" in December 1647 with Scotland's more moderate Covenanters, headed by James, Duke of Hamilton. They agreed to send an army to restore Charles in return for a royal promise to establish Presbyterianism in England for just three years. The Engagement also initiated a process whereby the Protestant and Catholic camps in Ireland—where war had continued ever since the 1641 rebellion—would unite by late 1648 behind the cause of a royal restoration.

The Engagement triggered the second civil war— a series of uncoordinated royalist uprisings in England and Wales in 1648. These were crushed by the army under Fairfax, while Cromwell smashed Hamilton's invading army at Preston in August. The victorious army was no longer in a mood for compromise with the king. In Pride's Purge on 6 December it excluded 200 or so MPs who favoured continued negotiations with Charles, leaving a "rump" of radical Independents to establish a high court of justice to try him for what they saw as his crime of inflicting civil war on the country.

Some officers already wanted Charles executed; others—Cromwell probably among them—were willing to spare him if he stood down his forces in Ireland. But, emboldened by this strong show of Irish support, Charles refused to recognise the court's authority, daring parliament to restore him or face the consequences.

His intransigence removed any lingering doubts in the minds of Cromwell and other regicides that the moment for justice against "that man of blood" had finally arrived. Charles was beheaded at Whitehall on 30 January 1649.

Opposite: Speaker William Lenthall (1591–1662) and his family, a painting of c. 1643–45 attributed to Edward Bower. Lenthall was famous for his resistance to Charles I's demands for five leading members of the Commons on 4 January 1642

John Pym, an engraving after Edward Bower, 1644

John Pym (1584–1643)

Pym was the unofficial leader of the Commons in the first part of the civil war, despite the fact that he was not wealthy (he owned a very modest amount of land in Somerset) and never held high office. By April 1640, when he took a leading part in voicing opposition to Charles I, he was a veteran of five parliaments. In each of them he sat by courtesy of aristocratic patrons. In the assemblies of the 1620s he criticised the king but was never subsequently singled out for retribution. He spent the 11 years when parliament did not meet in the 1630s in advancing various economic and puritan colonial ventures. When parliament was again summoned, in 1640, his skilful and persuasive oratory made him a natural leader of opposition in the Commons. From November that year he spearheaded attacks on almost every aspect of the 11 years' royal rule until an exasperated king attempted to arrest him and four other MPs in January 1642. Thereafter, Pym's aim was to set secure limits to the king's power.

After the outbreak of civil war, which Pym blamed on the king, he led the creation of a parliamentarian war effort, developing a range of administrative and fiscal measures, notably the excise tax (1643). Until his death he was pre-eminent in the committee of safety, the main executive committee devised by parliament to oversee this work. From 1641 he was lampooned as "King Pym" because of his dominance of politics. Recently, historians have questioned his independence of judgement and action, but he occupied an unrivalled position as a manager of parliamentary business because of his tireless capacity to work and his authority among fellow-parliamentarians.

In image text: DIT HVYS IS TE HVER. · THIS HOVSE IS TO LETT · Be gone you rogues you haue sate long enough · C: Cyper · C: Lam. · G. O. Cromwel. · This is an Oule.

Parliament, the law and the army, 1649–60

Shocking though it was, the execution of Charles I did nothing to resolve the crucial questions that were raised by the civil war and proceeded to dominate the so-called Interregnum. These concerned who was to rule the country and the institutions through which the country was ruled. The result was a remarkable period of constitutional experimentation. In January 1649, the "rump" of the House of Commons (the members who were left after Pride's Purge in December 1648) declared that it alone was the supreme power in England. It abolished the House of Lords and the monarchy, and established a council of state as the country's new executive. This was an institutional revolution driven by necessity, rather than idealism, reflecting a situation in which a tiny minority—the army and its supporters in the Rump—had overseen the execution of the king against the wishes of the vast majority of the population.

Nevertheless, the military and civilian politicians often had very different interests and concerns. Many of the soldiers wanted sweeping religious and social reforms to create a nation fit for (as they saw themselves) God's chosen people. Many MPs were more concerned with a return to political stability and the maintenance of religious and social order. With the army fully engaged until 1653 in subduing the external enemies of the English commonwealth—first the Irish and then the Scots —the sovereignty of the Rump remained unchallenged. But in April that year, the army having finally lost patience with its failure to enact wholesale reforms of religion and society, Cromwell forcibly dissolved the Rump Parliament.

In the hope of achieving such change, the army's commanders then devised a constitutional experiment that remains unique in English parliamentary history. Fearing (no

Above: A contemporary Dutch print showing Oliver Cromwell and his soldiers clearing the Rump Parliament out of the House of Commons chamber on 20 April 1653

"Cromwell was perhaps the only individual capable of maintaining the fragile alliance between the army and civilian supporters of the 1650s regimes"

doubt correctly) that free elections would return a parliament hostile to the commonwealth, the army, in consultation with its supporters among the religious sects, nominated 140 members to a new assembly. Meeting in July 1653, the "Barebones Parliament" —the name taken from its most wonderfully named member, Praise-God Barbon—was an uneasy mix of radical and more moderate voices. The extreme agenda of their colleagues eventually saw the moderates surrender the assembly's powers back to Cromwell in the following December.

Once again the army responded in innovative fashion. In the same month the army leadership— the council of officers—adopted England's first ever written constitution, the Instrument of Government. This installed Cromwell as Lord Protector of England, Scotland and Ireland. He was given power to issue "ordinances" that were binding in law until a new parliament met in September 1654. But, despite restrictions on who could serve as an MP and who could vote in elections, the first Protectorate Parliament proved disastrous for the new regime. Members challenged the legality of the Instrument. They threatened the future of the army by refusing

to vote adequate money for it. Cromwell's angry response was to dissolve the parliament in January 1655.

The army's disenchantment with parliaments, together with a royalist rising in the following March, contributed towards the imposition of direct military rule later that year. England and Wales were divided into 12 areas, each under the command of a military governor or major-general. Given the power to tax all former royalists, the major-generals were also charged with maintaining security and enforcing the army's long-desired moral reformation of society. Unsurprisingly, their rule proved deeply unpopular. When a second Protectorate Parliament was called in September 1656, even after the army excluded almost 100 MPs and around another 50 withdrew in protest, Cromwell still found himself pressurised into abandoning the experiment with the major-generals.

The case of James Naylor, a Quaker preacher whom parliament tried and severely punished for re-enacting Christ's entry into Jerusalem, showed up the divisions among the regime's supporters about religion and the maintenance of order. For many MPs, Naylor's (to them) blasphemous actions demonstrated the disorder that the state's *de facto* liberty of conscience positively encouraged. But Cromwell, who gave occasional support to the Quakers, was troubled by parliament's action. He asked by what authority they had acted as if they were a court of law. He received no answer.

What most MPs wanted was to recreate stable and conventional government. That aim was behind the attempt of leading civilian MPs to make Cromwell king through the provisions of a new written constitution, the Humble Petition and Advice. Although Cromwell eventually refused the offer of the crown, perhaps fearing the reaction of the army, the Humble Petition was formally adopted by parliament in May 1657. But if the document signalled a return to more traditional forms of government, settled government remained elusive. When parliament—which now included those members excluded in 1656 and an "Other House" (a sort of House of Lords) of 42 members—reconvened in January 1658, republican MPs openly challenged the "Other House".

Below: Cromwell was one of the first to sign the death warrant of Charles I in 1649

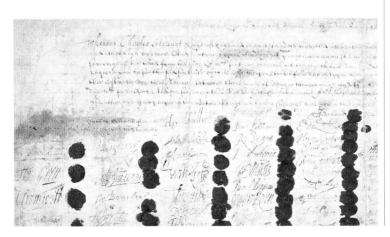

Oliver Cromwell (1599–1658)

Few politicians have sustained such a complex and ambivalent relationship with parliament as Oliver Cromwell. He was both its champion and its destroyer.

Born in Huntingdon, he was typical of the lesser East Anglian gentry. He played a part in the local government of his native town from 1624, accounting for his election there in 1628. He contributed little to the proceedings of the 1628–29 parliament, and little is known about his activities in the 1630s: there was nothing to suggest he was then actively hostile to the government of Charles I. Even his opposition to a project of major landowners to drain the East Anglian fens did not amount to much.

But around 1638 Cromwell underwent a religious conversion, and this puritan faith drove his career in the Long Parliament (1640–48), in which he represented Cambridge. He intervened early and effectively in that assembly, despite his relative inexperience. On the outbreak of civil war he combined sporadic but purposeful attendance in parliament with outstanding military leadership. He engineered the army reforms of 1644–45 and reached the high command of the New Model Army. In 1648, he tacitly supported the expulsion of MPs who sought compromise with the king, and led those who signed his death warrant. His own growing radicalism was not matched by the Rump Parliament (1648–53). In 1653, he used the army to topple it from power.

As head of state (1653–58) with the title of Lord Protector, he ruled under England's first and only written constitution. He planned for parliaments to continue to play a part, but with radicals and conservatives alike opposed to his new form of kingship, he struggled to create a government that was not based on military power. These intractable problems of state security and legitimacy persisted after his death.

*Oliver Cromwell: a miniature
by Samuel Cooper, 1649*

Within a matter of days, an exasperated Cromwell berated and then dissolved the parliament.

Cromwell was perhaps the only individual capable of maintaining the fragile alliance between the army and the civilian supporters of the 1650s regimes. His death in September 1658 removed the major obstacle to the return of the monarchy. His son and designated successor as Protector, Richard Cromwell, lacked the full backing of the army, having never been a soldier, and proved an ineffective leader. He lasted for nine months before being forced to recall the Rump Parliament and to resign.

The Rump's return to power was even more short lived when once again it failed to meet the army's expectations. It was expelled in October and the country reverted to a form of military rule under a committee of safety. Yet the officers' actions split the army. In a rapid series of momentous events, George Monck, commander of the forces in Scotland, disagreed with the Rump's removal and marched into England. Overcoming resistance he restored the Rump once again in December. In February 1660, he forced it to allow the members excluded in 1648 to be readmitted. The revived Long Parliament finally dissolved itself in March, having organised free elections, which saw the return in April of a pro-royalist Convention Parliament. Within a week, the Convention voted that the government should once again be by king, Lords and Commons, and invited Charles I's son, Charles II, to return from exile to take the throne.

The Interregnum constitutions

During the 1650s, the English Revolution produced the only formal written constitutions that Britain has ever had, and it is worth reflecting on how they adapted the old ways of government to new purposes. It was a curiously ad hoc affair. King Charles I had been executed for religious and political reasons rather than from a deep desire for constitutional change. The House of Commons claimed sovereignty by a short resolution on 4 January, primarily intended to justify the trial of the king. After the king's execution on the 30th there was an awkward pause.

Not that there was a shortage of ideas. Classical republicans argued for a settlement based on that of Ancient Rome, founded

Left: A print, probably published after the Restoration in 1660, depicting how Cromwell and his allies were trying to destroy not only the monarchy, but also religion and the law

"The five fractious parliaments of the 1620s aired issues arousing wide concern—wars; religious 'innovations'; legal and illegal taxation; 'arbitrary' imprisonment; monopolies; and corruption"

on notions of liberty and civic virtue. The army called for a written constitution, based on that outlined in The Agreement of the People—a radical document of 1647 created after a process of discussion among army officers and men, and strongly influenced by the ideas of the Leveller movement and its central figure, John Lilburne. Instead, parliament tackled the problem piecemeal. A new executive body, the council of state, was set up on 7 February; in mid-March, acts were passed to abolish monarchy and the House of Lords, and it was not until May that a short act was passed declaring England to be "a commonwealth and free state by the supreme authority of this nation, the representatives of the people in parliament". There was no substantive change to this position before the dissolution of the Rump Parliament in April 1653.

In December 1653, Britain acquired its first written constitution, the Instrument of Government. This was an army-influenced document, which gave executive power to a "single person"—Lord Protector Cromwell—and a small council. Parliament was limited to a legislative function, and even this was reduced, because the council was able to issue ordinances (legislative decrees) when parliament was not in session. The single chamber parliament was reduced in size to 460 MPs. Sixty of them would be elected in Ireland and Scotland, to create the first "union" parliament.

The Instrument of Government was unpopular, and the increasing influence of civilian advisers around Cromwell in the later 1650s brought pressure for a more broadly based settlement, based on the "ancient constitution" of king, Lords and Commons. The result was the "Remonstrance" introduced in parliament in February 1657, which offered Cromwell the crown, reduced the power of the council and promoted the role of parliament (not least by re-establishing an upper chamber, known as the "Other House", and reverting to the old system of electing MPs). A revised version of this document, the Humble Petition and Advice, was passed by the Commons

at the end of March and, although Cromwell rejected the crown, he accepted most of the other proposals. The document became law in June.

The Humble Petition was not a well-crafted constitution. There was confusion over some of the articles, and supporting legislation—including measures to ensure that Irish and Scottish MPs would still be able to sit at Westminster—was never passed. After Cromwell's death in 1658, these problems would beset his son, Richard, and did much to destabilise his own parliament and lead to his fall from power.

Parliament and the public in the 17th century

Over the 17th century, the number of people who were in some way involved in parliament and its politics grew. Steady inflation and population growth between about 1500 and 1640 increased significantly the number of eligible voters. In the counties, people of quite modest means now enjoyed the annual income of 40 shillings from their freehold land that entitled them to vote. In boroughs, disputed elections were often resolved by extending voting rights to all substantial householders, not just the few men who were involved in the town's government.

The phenomenal growth of London as an international trading and financial centre ruled by wealthy merchants—and of its neighbour Westminster as a fashionable social and legal hub dominated by nobles and lawyers—made both of them lively centres for political discussion and discontent. The explosive growth in printing already had potentially subversive implications under Tudor governments. From the 1620s, it was complemented by the wide circulation of handwritten newsletters.

Left: A late 17th-century print showing an argument in a coffee house—coffee houses were seen as centres for political discussion and dissent, and in the 1670s the government discussed suppressing them

In the 1640s, weekly newspapers (with local, national and international coverage) were added to the mixture. News and polemic also reached a non-literate audience through sermons, libels, ballads and the theatre.

Interest in politics was stimulated as the five fractious parliaments of the 1620s aired issues arousing wide concern—wars; religious "innovation"; legal and illegal taxation; "arbitrary" imprisonment; monopolies; and corruption and favourites at court. However, under the Long Parliament, sitting continuously from November 1640, parliamentary proceedings interacted with popular action and opinion to a degree that no one had previously imagined.

Huge demonstrations outside the Palace of Westminster were designed to intimidate members inside it. The House of Commons was overwhelmed from the outset with petitions about illegal taxation, the condition of the clergy and other local or personal grievances. Later on, it would be beset by people who had suffered damage to their property or possessions in the war, from injured or unpaid soldiers, and by radicals seeking far-reaching political change. Parliament, the king and the army produced printed declarations and statements to justify their actions to the people. Parliament celebrated victories and glossed defeats with nationwide fast days, prayers and official sermons. Declarations for domestic and foreign consumption were entrusted to propagandists like William Prynne and Henry Parker.

In time, the opposing Presbyterian and Independent factions would also justify their actions in print. The monarchy had censored publishing, and parliament tried to do so as well, but it could not stem the flow of information and opinion. As well as official reports of its votes and decisions, the public was able to read plenty of unofficial publications

Right: An engraving by Richard Gaywood, showing the king passing Westminster Abbey in procession, either before his coronation in April 1661 or to open parliament a few weeks later

Sold by C. Wildeberch at ye Globe in St Katherines

R. Gaywood fec

containing speeches by individual MPs and
(sometimes satirical) accounts of its activities.

Popular demonstrations contributed to the
overturning of rule by parliament and the restoration
of the monarchy in 1660. For a time afterwards, the
government was able to limit involvement in politics
by the public more effectively. But during the "Popish
Plot" and Exclusion crisis of the late 1670s and early
1680s, books, pamphlets, newspapers and cheap "libels"
on political subjects, mass demonstrations, lobbying
and campaigning by partisan politicians were again
commonplace in London. The newly fashionable
coffee-houses joined alehouses as arenas for political
talk and conspiracy. Whigs and Tories would organise
great meetings in the City, or processions in which
effigies of hate figures like the Pope were burnt.

After the Revolution of 1688, parliament
would continue to resist publishing full accounts
of its debates—though it did decide to distribute the
official formal record of its decisions. But its members
could no longer assume that it could easily discuss
the business of the country without the people as
a whole looking on and listening intently.

Elections in the 17th century

Under the Stuarts, procedures for holding elections
remained largely unchanged from those in the
Middle Ages. Knights of the shire were still chosen
by those who held freehold land worth 40 shillings.
The borough constituencies continued to use a
complicated range of franchises based variously on
civic office, freeman status, property, local taxes or
residence. Only between 1653 and 1658, under the
protectorate of Oliver Cromwell, were major changes
made. In England and Wales seats were redistributed
from smaller boroughs to the counties. A new property
qualification was introduced for all voters. Men who

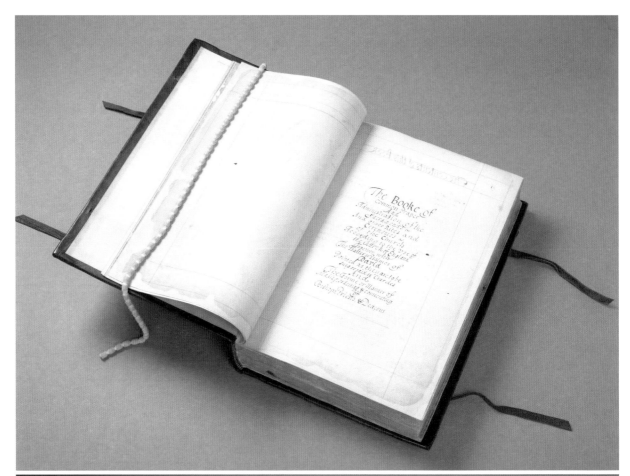

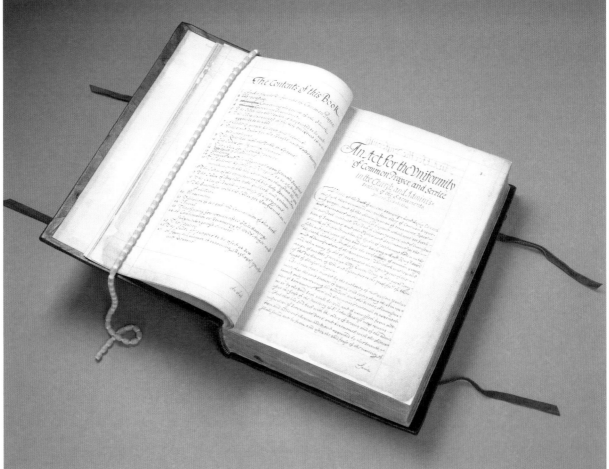

held real or personal property worth £200—wider in practice than many of the existing franchises —were able to vote. The old system was however reinstated with remarkably little fuss for the elections to the 1659 parliament. For those entitled to do so, the experience of voting remained much the same throughout.

But beyond these formalities, important change did take place. In 1604, in order to resolve a messy row over the Buckinghamshire election, James I tacitly conceded that the Commons, not the law courts, had the right to adjudicate election disputes while parliament was sitting. This was enough to give the Commons the power to decide who had the right to vote in a borough, when, as was often the case, that was a matter of argument. MPs rarely considered such matters impartially. The Committee of Privileges and Elections, where the disputes were debated, became known as "the most corrupt council in Christendom". The result was more influenced by partisan and personal considerations than by any principle. But MPs did tend to favour less restrictive franchises, which (along with inflation) helped bring about a modest expansion in the size of the overall electorate.

Elections themselves were becoming more partisan. Local and personal rivalries had always existed despite a strong preference to maintain unity within local society. But the ideological divisions of the civil war in the 1640s never really healed. Although over time the particular issues changed, by the 1680s they had morphed into the rivalry between "Whigs" and "Tories" over the Church and nonconformity, and over the right of the Catholic heir James to succeed to the throne. The deposition of a second Stuart king in 1688 then created as many new controversies as it solved. Elections became civil war by other means.

This influenced the management of elections. Although they remained the exception, contested elections were no longer as rare as they had once been. Fundamental rifts within county and urban communities were now less easy to conceal. Moreover, those local rifts were as likely to reflect national ones. The ubiquity of printed pamphlets and newspapers increasingly made it easier for voters to think of elections as national events deciding national issues. During the 1680s, the crown attempted to regain the initiative by repeatedly replacing borough charters. This was a way of altering franchises regardless of the Commons' wishes. It threatened to make the 1604 precedent irrelevant, but it often only heightened factional divisions within towns. By the end of the century what has been called "the rage of party" was in full swing.

Restoration to Glorious Revolution

Charles II's Restoration in May 1660 was a moment of relief and excitement for the many people who hoped for a return to political stability under traditional royal government. They were not to get it. The Convention Parliament, which called for the king to return, was replaced in 1661 by a new parliament, elected at the height of royalist enthusiasm. A high proportion of those elected had been enthusiastic supporters of the king, people who had intensely disliked the Interregnum regimes.

Known as "the Cavalier" Parliament, it provided heavy taxation to bail out a government left with a huge burden of debt by its predecessors. It was also persuaded to support the restored Church of England in its efforts to re-establish itself as the single national Church, and to introduce new laws to prevent nonconformists from setting up their own, alternative services.

Initially, struggles for power at the king's court did much to disrupt parliament. Furthermore, during the 1660s and 1670s, MPs became increasingly critical of the king's corrupt and expensive court. They were deeply unhappy too with the way that Charles II's policies were making England into a satellite to a powerful and expansionist France under Louis XIV. They were suspicious of the king's interest in suspending the laws on religious observance to allow nonconformists to worship publicly in their own way: they thought that this was intended to prepare the way for the toleration of Roman Catholics. The discovery that the king's brother and heir James had secretly himself become

a Catholic caused panic about a conspiracy to undermine England's religion, laws and liberties.

By the end of the 1670s, trust and cooperation between ordinary members of parliament and the government were already badly eroded. A series of ministers, especially the lord treasurer the Earl of Danby, tried to "manage" parliament by appointing key members to government posts or giving them grants and pensions. He also hoped that the government would become more popular by distancing the country's foreign policy from France and by giving strong backing to the Church.

The policy had only limited success. The grants and pensions were seen as more evidence of government corruption, the shift in foreign policy was undermined by Charles's continuing contacts with the French court, and the alliance with the Church was vigorously opposed by the political allies of the nonconformists. Danby's actions helped to bring into being a powerful coalition of opponents of the government. Its leaders included Anthony Ashley-Cooper, Earl of Shaftesbury, friend of the philosopher John Locke and former lord chancellor, who in a series of bold moves challenged Danby's policies. He and his allies associated the Catholic and French threats with the government's treatment of religious dissent and its desire to ignore and override political opposition. They aimed to conjure up nightmare visions of "popery and arbitrary government".

The "discovery" in 1678 of an alleged plot hatched by Catholics to bring down the government, kill the king and put his Catholic brother on the throne sent parliament and politics into their most dangerous crisis since the 1640s. The plot had been dreamed up by the disreputable, publicity-seeking adventurer Titus Oates and various associates, but it was widely believed, leading to the trials and execution of several innocent people.

Over the next three years, debate swirled round options to neutralise the threat of a Catholic successor to the throne and what it might do to the country's political and religious institutions. Political society seemed to be divided into two camps. One, the supporters of the established church and the defenders of James's right to become king, became known as

The draft of the Bill of Rights, showing final amendments agreed by both Houses on 12 February 1689

The Bill of Rights, 1689

The Bill of Rights is a key constitutional document for Britain. It was agreed to by King William III (1689–1702) and Mary II (1689–94) when they accepted the offer of the crown at the hands of the Convention Parliament in February 1689, following James II's defeat and escape to France at the end of 1688.

In a series of often very angry debates, both Houses had spent late January and early February arguing over whether James II could be formally replaced on the throne, and how they might ensure that the abuses of law and government during the 1680s could never happen again. The statement on which they finally agreed was originally called the "Declaration of Rights"; later it went through the normal procedures for creating an Act of Parliament, and became known as the "Bill of

Rights". It was not a constitution, but an assertion and confirmation of the ancient laws and liberties of the kingdom, underlining that many of the actions of James II and his predecessor, Charles II, had been arbitrary and illegal. The Scottish parliament, shortly afterwards, agreed a very similar document, the "Claim of Right", as they too decided to accept William and Mary as king and queen.

Both documents stated that it was illegal for the crown to try to suspend or dispense with the law, or to levy money without parliamentary assent, or to raise an army in peacetime, and insisted on due process in criminal trials. The Bill of Rights' vigorous assertion of the rights of the subject means that it is seen as parallel in importance with Magna Carta itself.

the Tories. The other, more hostile to the Church and friendly to nonconformists, demanded that James be shorn of power, and were labelled Whigs. Charles wavered enough in his approach to the problem to encourage MPs to believe that he could be persuaded to accept the exclusion of James from the throne: in fact, in 1681 he dissolved parliament and decided not to hold another rather than to bar his brother.

Over the next few years, Charles II called no more parliaments. He could only avoid them because of some timely financial support from the French government, a growth in his revenues that did not require parliamentary approval and a backlash against the Whigs. His death, in February 1685, meant the accession of the Catholic brother, as James II. James at first provided assurances about his commitment to the maintenance of the established Protestant Church. He summoned parliament, and indicated his willingness to observe the traditional forms of English government. But a major rebellion in western England, crushed severely in June, and the execution of its leader, Charles II's illegitimate son the Duke of Monmouth, made him less patient.

James was determined to repeal the "Test Acts" (the laws, passed in the reign of his brother, which made it illegal for Catholics to hold leading positions in the government). Ultimately, he hoped to bring back legal Catholic worship. The opposition aroused by his first attempt to repeal the "Test Acts" led him to dismiss parliament in November 1685, and to abandon his attempts to appease the Church and the Tories. He spent the next two years trying to pressurise politicians to accept his policies. He removed those who refused from their positions in local government. His "Declaration of Indulgence" of 1687 offering freedom of worship for all was vigorously opposed by the bishops. Many nonconformists rejected it too because its main aim was to achieve the return of Catholicism. Seven of the bishops were put on trial

in 1688 when they would not allow the Declaration to be read in the churches under their jurisdiction.

James's son-in-law, Prince William of Orange, the leader of the Dutch republic, was watching the development of James's policies and his authoritarian responses to his opponents with increasing alarm. He thought that if England became Catholic, it would almost certainly ally with France when France renewed its long military struggle with the Dutch, which had brought the republic almost to its knees in 1672. In November 1688, encouraged by some of James's domestic opponents, he led a Dutch force in an invasion of England.

Crippled by loss of morale and a defection of key commanders, including John Churchill, the later Duke of Marlborough, James's army crumbled. James himself fled to exile in France. Politicians assembled to try to decide what to do next. With William's agreement, a new parliament—the Convention—was called in January 1689. After bitter wrangling, it decided by February to offer the crown to William and his wife, James's daughter Mary.

Above: England's Memorial—a satirical and anti-Catholic print from 1688–89 celebrating the intervention in English politics by Prince William of Orange

Chapter four—
Oligarchy

The 1688 Revolution created a different type of state. It was still run by a monarch (or rather two of them, William and Mary) but, however much they and many politicians—especially Tories—disliked the idea, the monarch's title to the throne was effectively derived from parliamentary statute. Parliament, meeting for several months every year, was now a permanent presence, a proper institution. Without its active consent, it was impossible for kings to govern. England (soon to be Great Britain and then the United Kingdom, with the unions with Scotland in 1707 and Ireland in 1800) was now a parliamentary state. But how well did parliament really represent the country?

Contributors—
Robin Eagles
Stephen Farrell
Stuart Handley
Charles Littleton
Philip Salmon
Paul Seaward

The impact of the 1688 Revolution on England's parliament was profound. As a direct consequence of it the new monarchs, William III (1689–1702) and Mary II (1689–94) accepted some limitations of their traditional powers. They accepted the Bill of Rights, with its assertion of parliament's centrality to the processes of government. They agreed in the Triennial Act of 1694 that a new parliament should be elected every three years. But almost continuous war from 1689 to 1713 was as important as the Revolution itself in changing parliament.

William had come to England in part to secure backing for his wars with Louis XIV. The continual needs of the king and his successors to finance campaigns on the continent over close to a quarter of a century led to a revolution in the management of the economy, including the foundation of the Bank of England. Essential to this new and complex system of state finance was statute and parliamentary approval. The result was a significant growth in parliament's development as an institution. From 1689, parliament would meet every year.

These changes took place within a political structure in which the divide between Tories and Whigs had become entrenched. Monarchs, looking for solid support in parliament, had to take those divisions into account. Appointing ministers whom they trusted, but who could deliver that support, became a major preoccupation. During the 1690s the Whigs were dominated by a group of particularly committed politicians (the Junto). The Tories were in confusion after a Revolution that had forced them to choose between their loyalty to the king and their loyalty to the Church. In between were slippery court managers like the Earl of Sunderland and latterly a "Country" grouping (consisting of people who

rejected party labels altogether) mostly made up of discontented Whigs headed by politicians from two intertwined families, the Foleys and the Harleys.

William III attempted at first to construct a mixed ministry of Whigs and Tories and then wavered between Whig and Tory-dominated governments. Party conflict was embittered by accusations of corruption. Even the Commons Speaker, Sir John Trevor, was dismissed over charges of taking bribes; there were investigations into senior politicians on both sides, including Charles Montagu in the Commons (a Whig) and the Duke of Leeds and the Marquess of Normanby (both Tories) in the Lords.

Making these disputes more dangerous were the continued efforts of the supporters of the former dynasty (the Jacobites) to overturn the Revolution. In 1696, news of an assassination plot came to light, resulting in the arrest of Sir John Fenwick, one of James II's former generals. As there were not sufficient witnesses to enable the courts to proceed against him, Fenwick was tried before parliament, found guilty by act of attainder (a special, and ancient procedure avoiding the ordinary law courts, meaning that ordinary standards of proof were not required) and executed. Over the next half century, there would be many more Jacobite plots, real and imagined, the most serious in 1708, 1715 (the "fifteen") and finally in 1745 (the "forty-five"). The last, briefly, threatened the stability of the state before being crushed at the battle of Culloden.

The "rage of party" reached its zenith under Queen Anne (1702–14) as parliament grappled with concerns about the security of the Church of England, the succession to the throne, and the military campaigns waged against France by the Duke of Marlborough. Concerns about the safety of the Church initially provided a clear divide between

Opposite: The House of Commons, c. 1709–14, by Peter Tillemans. One of a pair with the painting of the House of Lords (overleaf)

"By leading the government from the lower House, Walpole's position helped to redirect power towards the Commons and away from the Lords"

Whigs, who broadly favoured greater toleration for nonconformist Protestants, and Tories, who attempted to force through a bill to stop dissenters avoiding the requirement that anyone holding public office should participate in Anglican Church services. It brought the Lords and Commons into conflict when a Tory majority in the Commons resorted to procedural sharp practice (known as "tacking") to stop the powerful Whigs in the Lords from voting it down.

In 1710, the Whig ministry attempted to impeach a Tory clergyman, Henry Sacheverell, for preaching against the Revolution. Although Sacheverell was found guilty, the trial revealed deep hostility to the Whigs in the country. Within months, Whigs were badly defeated in a general election, the ministry was out and was replaced by a new Tory-dominated coalition headed by Robert Harley, an adept, though deeply mistrusted politician, "Robin the Trickster" to his many enemies, who now headed an alliance of mostly Tories and some "court" Whigs.

None of Anne's children survived to adulthood. The fact created fresh uncertainty about the succession. The threat of a Jacobite revival and the return of a Catholic monarch put at risk the changes brought about by the Revolution. The Act of Settlement of 1701 had been designed to ensure that a Protestant would succeed when she died, determining the inheritance of the throne to the electors of Hanover, the German descendants of James I.

The Treaty and Act of Union with Scotland of 1707 was also motivated by the worry that if the two kingdoms were not formally united Scotland might succumb to the Jacobite Stuart line. Both acts further entrenched the power of the parliament of the newly minted Great Britain to deal with the highest matters

of state. Despite them, as Anne's death drew near in the summer of 1714, political tension built feverishly, with many politicians, including Harley (now Earl of Oxford) and the Secretary of State, Viscount Bolingbroke, anxiously (but discreetly) making contact with the Jacobite court in exile just in case power did not transfer peacefully to her continental cousins.

The 18th-century oligarchy and its opponents

In the event, the succession of George I (1714–27) passed off peacefully. It was helped by the increasing domination of politics by a relatively small number of men in the Lords and Commons, an oligarchy of wealth and privilege that had an immense stake in the peace and stability, and rapidly rising prosperity, of the country. It was also assisted by the refusal of the Jacobite heir (James Edward, the "Old Pretender") to give up his Catholic faith. Among those who felt excluded from the new regime were the Tories.

Suspicious of Tories like Viscount Bolingbroke and their perceived association with the Jacobites (especially after the rebellion of 1715), George I turned to the Whigs. For 50 years the Tories were shut out of political power, partly through the skill of the king's sure-footed minister, Robert Walpole, who made his office of first lord of the treasury the foundation for a career as Britain's first acknowledged prime minister. He was then able to remain in power after the death of George I and accession of George II (1727–60) thanks in part to the warm support of the equally astute new queen, Caroline (1727–37).

By leading the government from the lower House, Walpole's position helped to redirect power towards the Commons and away from the Lords. But this did not mean that the political system

Opposite: Queen Anne in
The House of Lords, c. 1709–14,
by Peter Tillemans

The Scottish parliament

The only known depiction of the Scottish parliament in session, probably engraved around 1685

Scotland's parliament had a history dating back at least to the late 13th century. Its origins, like those of England's, probably lay in the king's great council. As in England, the king would often use parliament to rally support such as in the 1320 Declaration of Arbroath. As in England, parliaments became the place where kings could get the consent they needed to tax the people. But there were many differences between the English and Scottish parliaments. Not unlike the English institution, the Scottish was based on the idea of "estates", an assembly of the different types of people in

society: the clergy, the nobles (who incorporated the lesser barons, the equivalent of "knights" in England), and the "commissioners" (like English burgesses) of the burghs, or towns.

But instead of meeting in separate chambers, as the English parliament had done since the 14th century, the Scottish parliament was a unicameral body. A key feature of the way it worked was the existence of a committee, known as the "lords of the articles", which would prepare the business of each session before the parliament itself discussed it. Some have seen this as making it easier for the crown to manipulate, but given the factions that existed within it, it did not always do this very effectively.

Having declined in importance during the 15th century, the Scottish parliament, like its counterpart in England, was at the centre of politics during the 16th century Reformation—particularly as the Scottish nobility fought for power after they deposed Queen Mary in 1567. But Mary's son, James VI (1567–1625, later James I of England, 1603–25), reasserted his power, avoiding parliament for 20 years. Parliament would again become a central institution as the Scots Covenanting movement wrested power from Charles I in 1639. From 1640 it would create a constitutional revolution, with its committees taking over executive power from the Scottish privy council. After defeat and occupation by the English army in the 1650s, and the Restoration of Charles II in 1660, the Scottish parliament would retreat to a more traditional and much weaker role as the Covenanting constitutional revolution was largely repealed.

The heyday of the Scottish parliament was perhaps in the last few years before its abolition. In the years after the fall of James VII and II from power in 1688 and his forfeiture of the throne in 1689 by the Claim of Right (a similar document to England's Bill of Rights) Scotland had its own deep political divisions, in some ways mirroring those in England. But parliament was at the centre of a vigorous political debate, a debate which, after 1702, became centred around the issue of a union with England. That the debate remained peaceful, and the outcome broadly accepted (despite Jacobite attempts to overturn it by violence, and some attempts to overturn it by politics) showed that parliament was now recognised as the authoritative place where the nation's future could be determined.

became any more "democratic". For a start, the Lords remained highly influential for much of the first half of the 18th century: most of the senior ministers were lords and individual peers exercised disproportionate influence over elections to the Commons. For another, Walpole and his allies, anxious to calm the "rage of party" as well as to entrench their own positions, were keen to limit opportunities to vote as much as possible.

The Septennial Act, passed in 1716, replaced the 1694 Triennial Act and restricted elections to one every seven years. Besides, because the population grew without any accompanying reform of the franchise, the proportion of those able to vote in elections fell. At the beginning of the century, about 23 per cent of all adult males possessed the right to vote; by the end of the century, the figure was under 17 per cent.

Walpole's premiership, sometimes dubbed "the Robinocracy", was not without opposition. Many saw it as based on systematic corruption of parliament and dishonesty, symbolised by his own enormous wealth. Standing against him was a coalition looking to George II's heir, Frederick, Prince of Wales, who was at the centre of a campaign that finally displaced Walpole in 1742. The prince died in 1751 before he could succeed to the throne. It was his son, George III (1760–1820) who did so, nine years later, determined to continue his father's work in trying to abolish parties (still often seen as groups of men whose private ambition threatened the public good) and rule as a "patriot king". He ended the proscription of the Tories, and he pulled Britain out of the Seven Years War (1756–63), in spite of a string of military successes, and to the dismay of many politicians, particularly the towering figure of William Pitt—"Pitt the Elder"—who, though not prime minister, had been both inspiration and strategist of the British war effort.

Despite his good intentions, George III, and especially his prime minister from 1762–63, his former tutor the Earl of Bute, were quickly seen as a threat to the liberty of the people and the integrity of parliament. The swift removal of several members of the former administration, among them the long-serving Duke of Newcastle, was referred to as the "massacre of the Pelhamite Innocents". The king's anti-party convictions encouraged others,

"Wilkes's campaign for the rights of his electors and freedom of the press left a lasting impression of the self-interestedness of those who led government and parliament"

notably the MP and philosopher Edmund Burke, to develop arguments justifying parties and stressing their value to a political system. The libertine MP John Wilkes was one of those who found cruder ways of responding to the new regime with more popular appeal.

Wilkes and liberty

Wilkes (1725–97) was notorious for his scandalous lifestyle before he entered parliament in 1757 as one of the members of a fraternity known as the Hellfire Club. It was not through parliament itself, but rather through journalism, that he made his political name.

He founded a weekly newspaper, the North Briton, in 1762, which he used for unrelenting attacks on George III's minister, Lord Bute, while trumpeting the freedom of the press.

In the famous issue 45, Wilkes turned his guns on the king himself over his determination to end the war. The government responded with a prosecution for seditious libel. Although Wilkes claimed parliamentary privilege—his right not to be arrested as an MP—he was expelled from the House of Commons and forced to seek refuge in France. Now identified with the cause of liberty but risking arrest and imprisonment, he returned from exile four years later in 1768, stood

Below: "Wilkes and Liberty" punchbowl, c. 1768, one of many commercially produced souvenirs celebrating Wilkes in the course of his long battle with the government and the House of Commons

Parliament and the press

The journalist William "Memory" Woodfall, 1745–1803, after Thomas Beach. Woodfall was one of the most successful publishers of parliamentary debates in the late 18th century

Members of parliament officially thought that their proceedings should remain private. It would be easier, they believed, to debate deeply controversial matters, such as how much tax to give to the king, without people knowing what they were up to, and constantly putting pressure on them to do something different.

In practice, many of them thought it might be quite helpful to their standing with their friends and electors to publicise their speeches and activities. Some, by the end of the 17th century, even felt that the public had a right to know what they were doing. In 1680 the House of Commons decided—in the midst of its confrontation with Charles II over the Popish Plot and the debates over the succession of the Charles's Catholic brother James—to print the daily record of its decisions, the Votes and Proceedings. But the House still disliked any accounts of its actual debates to appear in public, regularly punishing the publishers of newspapers who dared to print anything of the kind. One magazine resorted to disguising its reports as the debates of the Senate of Lilliput, Jonathan Swift's fictional country of small people, with Sir Robert Walpole not very well disguised as Flimnap.

The confrontation of the House of Commons with John Wilkes encouraged some of the publishers to challenge parliament directly. They became increasingly bold at printing their reports. In 1771, the Commons tried to summon them to the House for punishment. They evaded arrest, and with the help of Wilkes by virtue of his position as a London alderman, they turned the affair into a battle with the powerful corporation of London, provoking demonstrations in the streets outside Westminster, and a realisation among most MPs that the ban on reporting was no longer workable. Soon after, the Lords too conceded the point and stopped attempting to prosecute those publishing their debates.

Above: John Wilkes, by Robert Edge Pine, c. 1768. Wilkes was well-known for his squint, and regarded himself as unusually ugly

Opposite: The House of Commons, c. 1793, by Karl-Anton Hickel. William Pitt is speaking at the despatch box; his great rival Charles James Fox is visible on the lower row of seats opposite, wearing a black hat

for parliament again and was elected for Middlesex. Pressure from the government led to the Commons demanding a re-election and ultimately seating another candidate. Wilkes obtained his re-election on three occasions, secured feverish popular support, and created a formidable movement and powerbase in the City of London, being elected Lord Mayor in 1774. He was also returned to the Commons again the same year and this time was allowed to stay. The enormous interest generated by the case over more than a decade transformed the position over the reporting of parliament in the newspapers, helped to set off a movement for political reform and influenced

the developing arguments over the rights of the American colonies to political representation.

Wilkes's campaign for the rights of his electors and freedom of the press left a lasting impression of the self-interestedness of those who led government and parliament. It was one of several developments awakening an interest in parliamentary reform. Another was the difficulties arising out of Britain's now vast imperial and trading interests, especially its relations with the American colonies. The row with the colonists in the 1760s over how to pay for the defence of the empire raised hard and troubling questions about the right to be represented at Westminster.

The gradual slide into conflict with the Americans found parliamentarians divided in their views. Some—following the king and administration headed by Lord North—sought to impose British rule by force; others favoured a degree of compromise. Charles James Fox and his followers put their weight behind the Americans. A catastrophically badly fought campaign by the British forces, and the Americans' alliance with continental powers France and Spain, left the administration by 1783 with no choice but to concede defeat.

Defeat in a war fought across the globe—for a cause in which a good proportion of the population did not believe—resulted in a crisis of confidence in the English representative system. The arguments about taxation and representation in the 1760s and 1770s had encouraged people who lived in the great new industrial and manufacturing towns of the North to question why they sent no members to parliament, while tiny depopulated hamlets in the South, the so-called "rotten boroughs", where membership of parliament could change hands for money, did.

In 1776, John Wilkes (by then MP for Middlesex) made an impassioned plea in the Commons for reform of the franchise, pointing out the absurd arrangements of the present system. His efforts were followed in 1780 by the establishment of the Yorkshire Association under the leadership of the reverend Christopher Wyvill. There were also parallel demands for reform of government and the royal household (so-called Economical Reform) driven by Edmund Burke and a Whig faction led by the Marquess of Rockingham. Repeatedly, attempts to secure change were snubbed by the majority in the House of Commons. The young meteor politician, William Pitt (son of Pitt the Elder), who was appointed prime minister at the age of just 24 in the winter of 1783, started off as an advocate of reform. Only precariously in power and his enthusiasm

blunted by repeated failure, he abandoned the cause after the defeat of an attempt to introduce limited reform in 1785.

Abandonment of reform perpetuated many absurd abuses—the worst being the "rotten boroughs". Old Sarum, an uninhabited mound of ancient ruins near Salisbury, was the most famous of them. With their minuscule electorates and total control by local landowners, rotten boroughs were the most glaring anachronisms in Britain's unreformed electoral system, "cancerous carbuncles

"Peace would bring a post-war economic slump and a more radical, less genteel, demand for political change"

on the face of the constitution", as one contemporary put it. The 1832 Reform Act famously abolished 56 rotten boroughs, transferring their parliamentary seats to English counties and unrepresented northern industrial towns. Some of the more populous boroughs under the influence of local patrons remained, but the absurdity of two MPs being elected for places like Dunwich, a coastal town that had fallen into the sea, was now a thing of the past.

Rotten boroughs have inspired a string of savage political satires, from Thomas Peacock's "Borough of One-vote" electing an orangutan to Blackadder's antics at "Dunny-on-the-Wold". However, they were not without some redeeming features. Family-controlled boroughs provided many a leading politician with a youthful entry to the Commons, before they acquired the experience that would secure them more popular approval. They also offered a safe berth when things went awry. More significantly, however, the sale of seats by rotten borough owners made the Commons far more accessible to self-made men from non-elite backgrounds and various interest groups. Long before the official enfranchisement of Manchester, for instance, the cotton magnate Sir George Philips had unofficially represented the town, sitting as a "paying guest" for a series of rotten boroughs.

Reform postponed

The American war of independence had brought home the implications for domestic politics of inattention to the affairs of Britain's growing empire. In the 1780s, parliament would not only acquire direct responsibility for governing the affairs of India—in effect nationalising the huge monopolistic concern, the East India Company—it would also instigate a huge investigation into the way the company had conducted its business. From 1786, one of the Whig factions, led by the charismatic but unreliable Charles James Fox, attempted to make up for a dramatic loss of power to a regenerating Tory party under Pitt by trying to bring to book the East India Company's former governor of Bengal, Warren Hastings. In 1788, Hastings was impeached but the proceedings rapidly lost focus. As the Foxites became bogged down in prosecuting Hastings, Pitt was able to consolidate his position.

The affair was soon overtaken by the events of the French revolution in 1789. Welcomed at first by many as a sign that France was recognising the benefits of constitutional monarchy, British delight turned to horror as the revolution was hijacked by more radical elements, who executed their king and instituted a bloodbath. Pitt's government, fearing contagion at home, treated enthusiasm for reform as subversion and treason and implemented a series of repressive acts. Britain and France went to war in 1793. The conflict lasted, with one brief respite, for more than two decades. For all that time, the demand for change was suppressed while the British representative system became more embedded, more corrupt and more out of date.

Peace, after the final defeat of French emperor Napoleon I at the Battle of Waterloo in 1815, would bring a post-war economic slump and a more radical, less genteel, demand for political change. It was symbolised by the mass rallies in the new industrial

The office of Prime Minister in the 18th century

Sir Robert Walpole (left) talking to the Speaker, Sir Arthur Onslow, in the chamber c. 1728–42, after a painting by William Hogarth and Sir James Thornhill

One of the most significant political developments of the period was the emergence of the office of prime minister. Sir Robert Walpole (1722–42) is normally credited with being the first effective holder of the office, though Walpole never styled himself as such. He owed his position to holding in combination the offices of first lord of the treasury and chancellor of the exchequer, as well as being the principal government spokesman in the Commons. It was the first of these offices that was to become synonymous with the premiership. Walpole was notorious for presiding over a system based on corruption, but his significance was not so much the extent of his authority—it could be argued that the Earl of Godolphin (Lord High Treasurer from 1702–10) or Robert Harley (Lord High Treasurer from 1711–14) had wielded more extensive control over appointments—but his ability to maintain his position from the House of Commons for such a lengthy period. After Walpole's fall and following the short-lived ministry of the Earl of Wilmington, the effective inheritor of Walpole's mantle was Henry Pelham (1743–54), who again presided over the ministry from the Commons.

Government in the 18th century, though, remained a collaborative affair with the king at times a very active partner. During the remainder of the century, only three prime ministers managed the government from the lower House: George Grenville (1763–65), Lord North (1770–80) and William Pitt (1783–1801, 1804–06). The other eight were all senior figures in the House of Lords, though the Duke of Portland (1783) for one was merely a figurehead presiding over the so-called Fox-North coalition. Even in the nineteenth century many prime ministers led the government from the Lords: only in the twentieth century did it become the firm convention for the position to be held by an MP.

centres like Manchester, where a mishandled attempt at crowd control in 1819 resulted in the Peterloo massacre, a symbol of the instinct for repression of a threatened political elite. Though interest in reform waxed and waned over the next decade, the pressure by the early 1830s—increased by battles over the granting of political rights to Catholics in 1829—would become impossible to resist.

Parliament and a developing economy

Parliament in the 18th century encouraged the development of the economy through the passage of a huge number of acts that made it possible to undertake a whole range of measures for "improvement". Though they were passed by parliament, the initiative was local, coming from corporate bodies, groups or individuals. Legislation like this had been promoted for centuries before but, in the 18th century, the number of bills grew dramatically. The key to this development was the increasing predictability of the parliamentary session after 1688. As parliament met every year, usually in the winter months, it made it not only easier to plan legislation, but also more likely that it would actually get passed—rather than abandoned when a parliamentary session ended.

Most of these bills—referred to as "private" bills or acts to distinguish them from the public legislation that had much broader effects—were for specific local projects that needed the force of law. This was usually because they involved levying a tax or a toll on individuals, or setting up new institutions with coercive powers, such as the compulsory purchase of land. About 20 per cent of the acts passed between 1714 and 1800 related to improvement of the country's infrastructure. Seventy-five per cent of these related to turnpike roads.

By 1770 turnpikes covered 15,000 miles of road, administered by over 500 trusts. The trusts were empowered to levy tolls in order to raise funds for the construction and maintenance of the highway. In 1726, for example, the proposal for a bill to repair the road between Liverpool and Prescot said that the traffic in coal and also wool, cotton, malt and other goods had overwhelmed the customary methods of repairing the road. The bill named local notables as trustees, who were empowered to raise money by charging tolls so that they could invest in building new roads and maintaining old ones.

Other infrastructure acts helped with bridge building, harbour development, river navigation and the construction of canals. River navigation bills, like turnpike bills, had to allow the raising of money through tolls. But they also needed to compensate landowners for any loss of land or property rights as a result of measures to make the river easier to sail along—such as straightening the river channel or removing fishing weirs. Later in the century canals were similarly created with powers given by parliamentary legislation. Some port facilities like Liverpool's docks were developed under private acts, allowing the town's corporation to levy tolls on all shipping that used the port. Hull needed a bill in 1774 to authorise the use of land and customs revenue to fund the building of public quays and a dock.

Below: An engraving showing "The Sucking Worm Fire Engine", designed to promote an Act of Parliament to enable its use

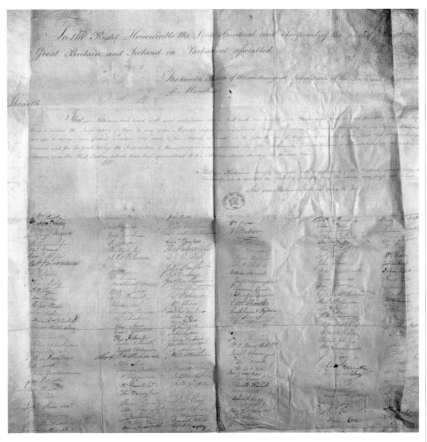

*Above: A petition to the House of
Lords from Manchester supporting
the bill for the abolition of the
slave trade, 1806*

to encourage mining, forestry or building developments. The acts would safeguard the interests of the family or provide compensation while they encouraged new economic activities.

To become an act of parliament, each piece of legislation had to be initiated by petition from the interested parties. They would be municipal bodies, groups of local men, or—in the case of estate acts —the individuals concerned. The process became more professional as the number of bills increased: local MPs would guide bills through the legislative process on behalf of their constituents, peers with local interests did the same in the Lords, and a body of agents emerged, specialising in drafting legislation and securing its passage through both houses of parliament.

The process involved long and often costly negotiation. Bills would sometimes be withdrawn after being introduced, and replaced by a better bill in the following session. In May 1720, for example, the Weaver Navigation bill was narrowly defeated in the House of Commons, but in the following session an improved bill passed without opposition. Often MPs were aware of local concerns and could address them as the bill went through parliament. Closely respecting property rights but relatively efficient in processing legislation, parliament provided a remarkably effective forum for resolving the conflicts of interest that naturally occurred in a period of rapid and extensive economic change.

Parliament and slavery

One key conflict would be over the issue of slavery, the use of which in the British colonies was an important contributor to the country's economy. Parliament's involvement with slavery remains a source of historical controversy and impassioned debate. For some, parliament as an institution stands condemned for fostering the legislative framework

But it was not just transport infrastructure that was the subject of private legislation. Improvements in many towns such as piped water supplies, paved streets and street lighting were financed in the same way. Enclosure acts allowed common fields to be taken into private ownership, resulting in improvements in productivity. There was also a huge number of private bills affecting individual estates. Most of these were intended to overcome particular legal difficulties affecting individuals or families. But some of them were in essence improvement acts: they might allow for the alteration of complex family legal settlements

Pitt and Fox

William Pitt ("Pitt the Younger", 1759–1806) and Charles James Fox (1749–1806) were the most famous and talented politicians of their time. They were also among the best connected. Both emerged from the highest ranks of the Whig party. Pitt was the son of another William Pitt ("the Elder"), a politician who had led Britain's global struggle in the Seven Years' War with France of 1756–63. Fox, a descendant of King Charles II, was the son of Henry Fox, a politician who had responded to a humiliating subordination to Pitt the elder in the House of Commons by helping George III to end the war after he gained the throne in 1760, and by supporting the new king's hated minister Lord Bute. Charles James Fox and Pitt the Younger were both hot-housed children, favourites of their fathers (his father's indulgence was said to have made Fox into an idle spendthrift, addicted to gambling and women).

Fox was elected to parliament in 1764 at the age of 19, despite the fact that men were not supposed to become MPs until they were 21. Twenty years later, deeply distrusted by royalty because of his support for the Americans in their war of independence, he was forced from office by the king. The replacement for his ministry in which he had been foreign secretary (the much-derided Fox-North coalition) was headed by Pitt, only 24, and elected to parliament just three years before. Shaky at first, Pitt remained premier continuously and exhaustingly until 1801, with a further period from 1804 until his death under two years later. For most of that time he faced Fox who, as the head of a Whig party, was dedicated to limiting the powers and prerogatives of the crown. The French Revolution of 1789 was greeted by Fox with enthusiasm as a blow to royal power in another country. But as the Revolution turned violent and bloody many in his party deserted him. Fox himself, while lamenting the atrocities, attempted to explain the excessive brutality as an understandable reaction to monarchical despotism.

From 1793 Britain was at war with France. Pitt, like his father, became a celebrated (though less successful) wartime leader. Fox, with a dwindling band of supporters, became associated with a growing radical movement, opposing a war that he believed to be unnecessary. Between 1797 and 1801, thoroughly disillusioned, he seceded from parliament altogether. Poles apart, the two men's differing political positions now reflected their apparently contrasting characters: Fox the brilliant but carefree playboy, Pitt the calculating political machine.

William Pitt (top) and Charles James Fox (bottom) by Robert Dighton, c. 1801

"Great Britain would become, over the following century, the world's leading industrial and commercial power, the 'workshop of the world', with a growing empire"

that supported the Atlantic slave trade, particularly between the 17th and 19th centuries. Merchants who were MPs lobbied in defence of their commercial interests, and slave owners shared in the total compensation of £20 million granted to them by parliament when their slaves were freed in 1833.

For others, parliament lies at the heart of the story of a determined struggle over decades by the MP William Wilberforce and the campaigner Thomas Clarkson. Mobilising opinion outside parliament, they tried to persuade ministers and MPs to agree to bills to abolish the slave trade and to emancipate the slaves in the British colonies. Those bills were eventually passed in 1807 and 1833, respectively. For much of human history, slavery was accepted, including by parliamentarians, as a fact of life. However, the vast human misery caused by the forced transportation of millions of Africans to be slaves in the Americas has long been generally recognised, and parliament acknowledged slavery's inhumanity when it ended the slave trade in 1807.

Making the United Kingdom

The two kingdoms of England and Scotland had shared a monarch since 1603 when James VI of Scotland inherited the English throne as James I, the first representative of the Stuart dynasty to rule in England. A succession of Stuart monarchs—James I in 1604–07, Charles II in 1669–70, William III in 1689 and Anne in 1702–03—had all tried, but failed, to effect some sort of more permanent political union between their kingdoms. Under the Protectorate of Oliver Cromwell in 1654 the two kingdoms were

formally united, though this was only after the military defeat of the Scots, and it was backed by the presence of the English army. The two countries became separate again at the Restoration in 1660.

At the beginning of the 18th century the two kingdoms seemed to be drifting further apart. The cause was Scottish anger over the continued exclusion of its merchants from English trading markets and the question of who would succeed to the throne when the last of the Stuart monarchs, Queen Anne, died. In 1704, Scotland's own parliament passed the Act of Security, which declared its right to choose a successor to Queen Anne independent of whatever choice England made. They refused to vote funds necessary to Scotland's part in the ongoing war against France unless the controversial bill was approved by the queen. The English parliament retaliated by passing in March 1705 the Aliens Act, which proclaimed that England's northern neighbours, despite being subjects of the same monarch, were nevertheless "aliens" whose trade into England would be further restricted and in some cases prohibited.

The situation was dangerous, particularly in the context of war with France. To avert what appeared to be an escalating conflict between the two kingdoms, commissioners for each hammered out a treaty of political union between April and July 1706. The English and Scottish parliaments spent their respective sessions in 1706–07 debating, often heatedly, and eventually ratifying this treaty. By the ensuing Act of Union of March 1707 Scotland maintained its own legal system and its Presbyterian kirk (or church), and it gained the right of free trade to England and its colonies. But the northern kingdom did lose its ancient parliament. Henceforth the Scottish counties and burghs were to send 45 MPs and 16 "representative" peers—a far lower number than had sat in

Mrⁱ PERCEVAL Assassinated in the Lobby of the House of Commons by IOHN BELLINGHAM May 1ᵗʰ 1812

A contemporary illustration of the assassination

The assassination of
Spencer Perceval

At about 5 pm on 11 May 1812, the 49-year-old prime minister, Spencer Perceval—barrister, evangelical Christian and father of a large family—entered the lobby of the House of Commons in the old (pre-fire) Palace of Westminster. According to the parliamentary reporter William Jerdan: "there was an instant noise … I saw a small curling wreath of smoke rise above his head … I saw him reel back against the ledge on the inside of the door … and then … I saw him totter forward … and drop dead between the four pillars which stood there in the centre of the space, with a slight trace of blood issuing from his lips."

Perceval, who had been member for Northampton since 1796 and head of the Tory government since 1809, had been shot through the heart with a pistol. Before he died, he apparently called out, "Murder!" or "I am murdered!" His deranged killer, John Bellingham, a bankrupt merchant, was arrested in the commotion that followed, but offered no resistance. Although there were fears that his action was politically motivated, his only defence was that the government had failed to redress his grievances about being imprisoned for debt in Russia. He was executed a week later.

Perceval is not the only politician to have met a violent death on the parliamentary estate—the Conservative MP Airey Neave was killed by a car bomb on 30 March 1979—but he is the only UK premier ever to have been assassinated.

Right: *The Irish House of Commons in 1780, by Francis Wheatley*

the Scottish Parliament—to Westminster for the ensuing parliaments of what was now a new state, "Great Britain".

Great Britain would become, over the following century, the world's leading industrial and commercial power, the "workshop of the world", with a growing empire—despite the loss of part of it with the secession of the American colonies under the Treaty of Paris of 1783 after the American War of Independence. Most of these far-flung territories would remain separate from the kingdom itself, but the oldest and closest of Britain's colonies, Ireland, was brought within it right at the beginning of the 19th century. By an Act of Union with Ireland, the United Kingdom of Great Britain and Ireland came into existence on 1 January 1801.

Unlike Scotland, which had entered into its negotiations as an independent and separate kingdom, Ireland had been directly ruled by England since the 16th century. The English king's viceroy, the lord lieutenant, ruled with the close collaboration of a wealthy Protestant elite which had strong connections to England, over a population that remained largely Roman Catholic in religion.

Ireland had had a separate parliament since the Middle Ages. It was dominated by the Protestant elite, but its powers were severely limited. "Poynings' Law" for three centuries provided that the Irish parliament could not initiate legislation without the prior approval of the privy council in Westminster, and the Declaratory Act of 1720 insisted that laws passed by the Westminster parliament applied equally to Ireland. Change came towards the end of the 18th century as Irish MPs became increasingly resentful of these limits to their own legislative independence. In 1782, both Poynings'

Law and the Declaratory Act were repealed by the British Parliament. The Irish parliament—known as "Grattan's Parliament" after its most influential member—followed with a series of reforms using its new powers. It oversaw the abolition of restrictions on Irish commerce and admitted Catholics to the parliamentary franchise in 1793. But although the Irish legislature was now able to decide on its own laws, it did not control the country's executive, which took direction from London. This period of substantial Irish self-government was in any case soon brought to an end by the bloody Irish rebellion of 1798.

Many of the radical ideas of the French Revolution had had a receptive audience in Ireland. When Britain found itself in a long war with revolutionary France, a large and dangerous revolt in the island in the spring of 1798, supported by the French, gained many followers. It was put down by the British and much of the Protestant establishment in Ireland with a good deal of brutality.

In its wake, the British government saw Union with Ireland as the best way to prevent further disturbance. It used bribery and promises of patronage on an unprecedented scale in order to ensure that the parliaments of Westminster and Dublin (the latter of which had initially rejected the bill) both passed the Act of Union in the summer of 1800. The act provided that, from 1 January 1801, the parliament of the new United Kingdom of Great Britain and Ireland would contain 100 MPs representing Irish constituencies in the Commons, bringing the total there to 658, while 28 Irish representative peers, sitting for life, and four bishops of the established Church of Ireland, each serving for a session in rotation, would join the House of Lords.

THE LADIES CANDIDATE

Vote for
Darling
and
Parliamentary
BALLS
Once a Week

The Friends
of
Sir Charles
Darling
are requested to
meet this Eve
in the Assembly
Rooms — The Honble
Mrs Manley in
the Chair
Tea & Coffee at
7 o'Clock

Chapter five—
Building democracy

For most of its history, parliament and democracy were very different things. It was a small minority who could take direct part in electing the men who were supposed to represent the country. Most of parliament's members shied away from the idea of popular government, thinking it meant mob rule and threatened their wealth and property. The process of transition to democracy was slow and complicated. It took almost a century of reform, from 1832 to 1928, before all adults were able to vote on equal terms. The beginnings of the process coincided with the destruction of the medieval palace of Westminster by fire, and the creation of a dramatic new palace for representative government on the banks of the Thames.

Contributors—
Stephen Ball
Henry Miller
James Owen
Kathryn Rix
Philip Salmon
Caroline Shenton
Mari Takayanagi

A series of landmark legislative reforms in the 19th and early 20th centuries transformed Britain from a political nation whose parliamentary representation was dominated by a landed male elite to a modern democratic society, in which both men and women had the right to vote at elections and to sit in the House of Commons.

The First or Great Reform Act was passed in 1832 following mounting pressure for parliamentary reform. There had been rioting in a number of towns including Nottingham and Bristol after the House of Lords rejected a reform bill in October 1831. The Whig ministry of Earl Grey had taken office after the refusal of the Duke of Wellington's Tory administration to consider reform. Grey and his colleagues recognised the need for a limited measure to strengthen the existing constitution by removing some of the worst defects of the electoral system and better representing the diversity of national interests.

Their emphasis was not on creating a democracy; instead they wished to represent "the property, the wealth, the intelligence and the industry of the country". The existing jumble of franchises in the boroughs was replaced by giving the vote to all householders who occupied—either as owner or tenant—any property worth £10 a year or more. (In a few constituencies, such as Preston, this in fact proved less democratic than the old franchise.) New property-based qualifications were added in the counties. The electorate in Britain and Ireland increased from around 500,000 to around 800,000.

More significant than the change in the franchise was the redistribution of seats. Over 140 seats were reallocated, with previously unrepresented industrial centres such as Birmingham, Leeds and Manchester receiving two seats each, while "rotten boroughs" such as Old Sarum were stripped of their representation. Extra seats were also granted to the counties, in the belief that they would best reflect respectable propertied opinion. Despite these changes, dozens of "nomination" or "pocket" boroughs survived where MPs were effectively selected by a patron, usually the major local landowner. The beneficiaries of this included William Gladstone, who first entered parliament

Right: The House of Commons, 1833, by Sir George Hayter

Illustration of the fire from a broadsheet produced in London the following day

The fire of 1834

By the late Hanoverian period, the ancient buildings of the Palace of Westminster where parliament had sat for centuries had become an accident waiting to happen. The long-overdue catastrophe finally occurred on 16 October 1834 when a chimney fire caused by the unsupervised burning of wooden tally sticks (a form of medieval tax receipt) set fire to the House of Lords. Warning signs were persistently ignored, leading the prime minister later to declare the disaster "one of the greatest instances of stupidity upon record". A huge fireball exploded out of the building at around 6.30 pm, lighting up the sky over London, and immediately attracting thousands of spectators.

It turned into the most significant blaze between the Great Fire of London in 1666 and the 1940 Blitz, burning fiercely for the rest of the night. When the sun rose the next day it revealed a shattered and smoking collection of buildings. Most of them were cleared in the months that followed and the stone sold to salvage merchants or pushed into the river. Only Westminster Hall, the Undercroft Chapel of St Mary and part of the Cloister remain today of the survivors of 1834. Later commentators saw it as symbolic of the constitutional changes brought about by the Great Reform Act of 1832. At the time people were more likely to have seen it as divine judgement for the passing of the Poor Law Amendment Act of 1834, against which Dickens—a parliamentary reporter at the time of the fire—railed in *Oliver Twist*.

Above: Thomas Slingsby Duncombe MP presenting the Chartists' petition 2 May 1842 in the temporary House of Commons, the former chamber of the House of Lords

in 1832 as MP for Newark, a constituency that was controlled by the Duke of Newcastle.

Given the limited extension of the franchise, it was hardly surprising that hopes that the 1832 act would prove enough to satisfy the demand for change were forlorn. In the late 1830s and 1840s, the Chartists campaigned for further legislation, including universal male suffrage, equal-sized constituencies and the secret ballot. These demands went unmet by the next major instalment of reform,

in 1867, whose main purpose was to enfranchise "respectable" working men, giving the vote in boroughs to all householders and to lodgers who paid over £10 annually in rent. Although the Liberal party was more favourable to this change, it was a Conservative ministry led by the Earl of Derby and Benjamin Disraeli that passed the Second Reform Act. The electorate almost doubled, but there was less extensive redistribution of seats than in 1832.

The 1867 act had made little change to the county franchise but, as Britain's towns expanded into rural areas, the existence of differing franchises for county and borough voters seemed increasingly artificial. This was changed by the Third Reform Act of 1884–85, passed by Gladstone's Liberal ministry, but with considerable input from the Conservative leadership. The Conservatives were keen that the extension of the franchise should be accompanied by a substantial redistribution of seats, without which they feared the Liberals would reap a considerable electoral advantage. Over two million voters joined the three million already on the electoral register.

Even more significant was the complete redrawing of the electoral map. Whereas the majority of constituencies had previously returned two MPs, the Third Reform Act divided the country into largely single-member constituencies. Rather than being concerned to represent particular interests, representation was granted in line with population: the largest electorate was now eight times, rather than 250 times, the size of the smallest. The Third Reform Act ironed out many of the electoral system's inequalities, and, for the first time, dealt with Scotland and Ireland on the same basis as England and Wales.

Despite these major changes, Britain remained far from democratic. Not only were women excluded from the franchise, but so too were around 40 per cent of adult men. The strict residence requirements

*Right: The new Palace
of Westminster, 1851, by
E. Walker after Charles Barry*

and the complexities of the registration process, with claims to vote considered annually in the registration courts introduced in 1832, meant that many men failed to qualify; one Liberal MP described the British system as "democracy tempered by registration". The emphasis in accounts of the Fourth Reform Act of 1918 has been on the granting of the vote to women in the wake of the activities of the women's suffrage campaign and the upheaval of the First World War. But equally important was the need to prevent the potential political exclusion of men who had fought for their country.

After the 1918 reforms, which almost trebled the electorate and again redistributed seats in line with population, virtually all adult men possessed the vote, but the female franchise was restricted to those aged over 30. The 1928 Equal Franchise Act finally granted the same voting rights to men and women. Other alterations made in 1918 should not be overlooked: for the first time, all election contests throughout the country took place on the same day; the official costs of elections (such as returning officers' fees) were paid from public funds rather than candidates' pockets; and the complicated system of registration was replaced with the modern electoral roll.

Although hugely significant, these four acts do not fully explain the evolution of the modern British political system. The introduction of the secret ballot in 1872 was a key change, designed to protect newly enfranchised working-class voters from intimidation and influence. However, electoral corruption remained a sizeable problem. The 1883 Corrupt Practices Act therefore placed strict limits on how much candidates

could spend at elections. While this did not completely eradicate bribery and other misdemeanours, it made a marked improvement. Important steps in widening the pool of potential parliamentary candidates came with the abolition of the property qualification for MPs in 1858 and the introduction of payment of MPs in 1911, the latter a concession by the Liberals to the embryonic Labour party. Rather than being part of an inevitable and inexorable progress towards democracy, many of the features which we take for granted as part of the modern British democratic state emerged, like these, in a gradual and piecemeal fashion.

The new Houses of Parliament

The Victorian palace known as the new Houses of Parliament is one of the most famous buildings in the world. A masterpiece of early Victorian architecture and a spectacular feat of civil engineering, today it is a much-loved landmark on the London skyline. Its creation, however, was a tortuous business. Following the fire of 1834, the government had originally planned that the reconstruction would be undertaken on modest terms by Robert Smirke, its in-house architect. The press and public opinion demanded otherwise, and instead there was a public competition to find a new design for the nation's legislature, in the "Gothic or Elizabethan" style.

Ninety-seven entries were received, and number 64, identified only by a portcullis symbol, was eventually chosen as being superior to all the others. Its creators were Charles Barry (1795–1860) and Augustus Welby Northmore Pugin (1812–52). Barry, the son of a Westminster stationer, had grown up in the shadow of the old Palace and was a highly successful architect much sought-after in Whig circles. Pugin, as brilliant a polemicist for the Gothic revival as he was a designer, was himself the son of a well-known illustrator and artist. Together, they created the most famous building in the United Kingdom, but not without enormous struggle and constant setbacks.

Following the death of both men (it is not too much of an exaggeration to say the strain of work on the Palace eventually killed them both) their sons had a vicious public quarrel about who was responsible for the design. Today, it is recognised that this was a collaboration of two geniuses who brought complementary skills to an enormous enterprise. Barry's was the guiding hand in the design; and in addition he was a master planner, brilliant business manager and skilled political negotiator. Pugin provided the exquisite and inspirational detailing of the building's interior and exterior, and designed the spectacular effects of the House of Lords throne and the famous Clock Tower.

The practical challenges, even by the standards of Victorian invention, were immense. The new building was required to cover eight acres of unstable gravel beds. Its river frontage, a quarter of a mile long, had to be constructed in the treacherous currents of the Thames by means of an innovative cofferdam. Its towers were so gigantic they required feats of engineering and building technology never seen before, in order to construct it on the cramped site. The roofs were tiled in cast iron to fireproof the building, steam engines were used to transport materials across the scaffolding, and the interior design demanded craft techniques some of which had not been used since the middle ages. All of this had to be done while the business of parliament continued on site. There was a disastrous strike, plans for ventilation that would have blown the Palace sky-high, the stonework began to decay in the polluted air of London even before the building was finished, and the Great Bell—Big Ben—broke not once, but twice.

"Together, Barry and Pugin created the most famous building in the United Kingdom, but not without enormous struggle and constant setbacks"

Charles Barry's political difficulties were just as overwhelming. There was an immediate row from the disappointed competitors after he won. Both the government and the MPs proved exhausting, fractious and opinionated clients, frequently at war with each other and among themselves. Battling the interference of MPs, fending off the mad schemes of a host of crackpot inventors and busybodies, and despite the project coming in three times over budget and 24 years behind schedule, Barry eventually won through—though at great cost to himself, and to Pugin, both professionally and personally. Following Barry's death in 1860, work to complete the Palace of Westminster continued for the next 10 years under the direction of his son, Edward.

Although today the Houses of Parliament are regarded by many as the quintessential expression of Victorian Gothic architecture, in fact they owe much more to ideas about the "picturesque" of the late Romantic period, rather than to the Victorian theories of John Ruskin and his followers. Pugin is said to have told a friend wryly that the design was "Tudor details on a Classic body". Constructed during the age of the Chartists, the Anti-Corn Law League, the Irish potato famine, the railways and the Crimean war, this was the greatest building programme in Britain since the Middle Ages. It produced nothing less than a secular cathedral to modern representative government.

The party system, 1832–1918

One of the most remarkable political developments of the 19th century was the emergence of distinct political parties. The rise of a recognisably modern party system, though, was far from a smooth process and was shaped by changes both inside and outside the House of Commons.

The fierce debates surrounding parliamentary reform between 1830 and 1832 created a marked division inside the Commons. A coalition of Whigs, Radicals and reforming Tories, known collectively as Reformers, faced the remainder of the Tories, often referred to as anti-Reformers. This neat distinction did not last. Although the Reformers secured a huge majority at the 1832 general election, there were significant tensions between Whigs and Radicals. Loyalty to the government was weak. After the Whig-led administration of Earl Grey suffered a series of defections, King William IV controversially replaced them in November 1834 with a minority Tory ministry. Robert Peel, the new prime minister, subsequently issued the Tamworth Manifesto, outlining a more enlightened policy for the "Conservative" party, the name by which the Tories increasingly became known.

The Conservatives' failure to gain a majority at the 1835 general election, however, prompted the king to recall the Whigs, strengthened by a "compact" with the Irish MPs, led by the charismatic Daniel O'Connell. For the following 10 years, the Commons was effectively divided into two broad parties: Whigs, sometimes referred to as "Liberals", and Conservatives. Very few MPs changed sides and it was now increasingly accepted that parliamentary parties were the chief basis of governments.

The change was mirrored outside the Commons. In London, new political clubs were established: the Carlton for the Conservatives in 1832 and the Reform for the Whigs in 1836. In the constituencies, parties formed local registration societies to ensure their supporters were placed on the electoral register introduced by the 1832 Reform Act. Developments at local level, especially in the annual town council elections established in 1835, also helped to orient the politics of the parish around the parties.

Nevertheless, at elections, some candidates remained reluctant to adopt party labels. The idea that MPs were "independent" of party or government was still one that attracted many electors. The formation of a government, moreover, was still determined more by events inside the House of Commons than by the choice of the electorate at a general election.

This was especially the case in the years between 1845 and 1859, a period of great flux in the party system. The decision of Tory premier Peel to support the repeal of the Corn Laws (legislation which limited the import of grain in order to keep its price high for the benefit of farmers, but making bread more expensive for the poor) outraged a number of protectionists within his own party. Under the leadership of Lord George Bentinck and Benjamin Disraeli they deserted him and brought down his Conservative ministry in June 1846. The subsequent Whig government, led by Lord John Russell, relied heavily for its survival on the support of the "Peelites", a distinct group of backbench Conservatives who had supported Peel in repealing the Corn Laws.

The defection of many Irish MPs from the alliance with the Whigs in 1850 and disagreements between Russell and his foreign secretary Lord Palmerston further undermined the stability of the Whig government, and it collapsed in 1852. This confusion in party alignments was reflected by the subsequent establishment of a short-lived minority Conservative government, under Lord Derby, followed by a coalition government, led by Lord Aberdeen. It was not until June 1859, when, at a key meeting at Willis's Rooms in London, Whigs, Peelites and Radicals came together to form the "Liberal Party", that a sense of order was restored to the party system.

Following the 1867 Reform Act, there was a concerted attempt to harness the voting power of an increased electorate through the establishment of extra-parliamentary party organisations based on individual membership. Formed in 1867, the National Union of Conservative and Constitutional Associations generated affiliated associations across the country. In 1883, the Primrose League was founded to enlist the support of voters and non-voters, including women, for the Conservative cause. In 1877, Joseph Chamberlain established the National Liberal Federation, an ambitious project to spread the model of the Birmingham Liberal Association, which gave Liberal voters a role in choosing local committees to select parliamentary candidates. The connection between an MP and his party therefore became stronger. At the same time, MPs became ever more reliant on national party campaigns, with pamphlets, posters and election meetings gradually supplanting their own personal political campaigns.

Tighter party discipline was also evident inside the Commons by the 1880s. The growing demands made by governments upon MPs gave greater significance to the role of the party whips, who became increasingly less tolerant of non-attendance or revolt. The age of what conservative prime minister Lord Salisbury described as "the old type of Member who sat rather loose to his party" was coming to an end.

The rise of a distinct two-party system, however, was again interrupted by a controversial political issue: the Home Rule crisis of 1886. Gladstone's decision to support the restoration of legislative independence for Ireland led to a split in the Liberal Party and the formation of the Liberal Unionists, which at first had a significant backbench following and a separate national organisation until 1911. Paradoxically though, the divide on Home Rule drove both the Liberals and Conservatives towards greater cohesion and discipline, as maintaining party majorities inside the Commons became paramount.

The emergence in the third quarter of the 19th century of a labour movement intent on securing the election of working-class MPs also had a mixed impact on the party system. The 1885 general election witnessed the return of 12 working-class MPs, but they viewed themselves as Liberals, and were known, at first pejoratively, as "Lib–Labs". The embryonic "Labour Party" made a small electoral breakthrough in 1906, when 29 of its

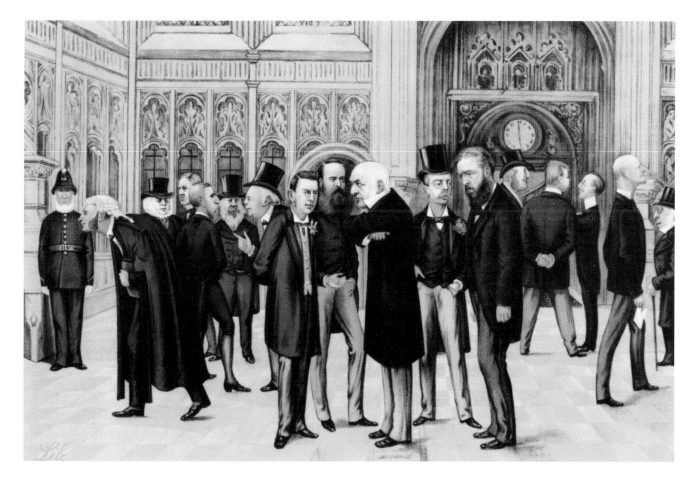

candidates were returned, but this was largely the result of a secret pact made between Ramsay MacDonald and the Liberal chief whip Herbert Gladstone, whereby Liberals would not oppose Labour candidates. The prospect of the Labour Party emerging as a potential party of government, therefore, was far from certain on the eve of the First World War.

What was clear, though, was that by the beginning of the 20th century, a recognisably modern party system had emerged, where voters polled for candidates of nationally organised parties led by a potential prime minister.

Elections in 19th-century Britain

The 19th century witnessed some of the greatest changes of any period to the United Kingdom's system of electing MPs. Bar the anomaly of women still being unable to vote, by 1900 most of the key features associated with modern elections—secret voting, single member constituencies, first-past-the-post polls, mass electorates, party-based election campaigns—were all in place.

The contrast with the electoral system in 1800 could not have been more marked. Only limited

Above: "The Rights of Women";
an 1853 print by George
Cruikshank imagining the effect
of enfranchising women, with
the "Ladies' candidate" attracting
the adulation and all of the votes

"Bar the anomaly of women still being unable to vote, by 1900 most of the key features associated with modern elections were all in place"

for a borough election to £5,000 for a county seat, the equivalent of hundreds of thousands today.

By far the most striking change, however, was that before 1872 all voting was performed in public, viva voce, rather than in secret. Even non-electors frequently played an active and noisy part in attempting to influence those with the vote, in what amounted to a form of indirect representation. As one candidate suggested in 1841, "The vote is public property, the elector is only a trustee, and you, the non-electors, have the right to scrutinise and to direct the exercise of the voters' function". Methods used could range from threats to boycott certain traders or businesses to more subtle forms of persuasion. "If the men have the votes, the women have the influence," quipped the future prime minister Disraeli in his novel *The Election*. The prevalence of double member seats meant that many electors ended up casting one of their votes for principle and the other to satisfy a local interest.

Non-electors also participated in the public theatre of the nomination and declaration, usually staged on a makeshift wooden hustings before a large crowd. The ceremony of the "show of hands" for each candidate, in particular, enabled the unenfranchised to make their presence felt. A difference between the "popular" opinion expressed at such events and the outcome of the poll was often the catalyst for trouble. Not that the participants needed much of an excuse. Grand processions of rival supporters, accompanied by banners and marching bands, and rituals such as the chairing ceremony, where newly elected MPs were forcibly paraded around in lavishly decorated seats, before the chair was broken to pieces, more or less sanctioned a degree of violence.

Free drink supplied by the candidates also fuelled tensions, though it was usually consumed in such vast quantities that it ultimately had the opposite effect. In 1835, one provincial newspaper dryly noted how an unfortunate Derbyshire elector had been unable to vote, after drinking "at Tory orgies till abused nature revolted", whereupon "the drunkard retired to the privy to relieve his stomach, but being unable to keep his equilibrium, pitched head first into the disgusting receptacle, where he stuck fast by the shoulders in the seat and remained for several hours".

Pre-democratic elections were therefore surprisingly participatory. But rather than being centred around national

numbers could vote in most early and even mid-19th-century elections. In addition, the fact that so many constituencies elected two (or more) MPs meant that it was not unusual for elections to be decided without a poll—if the number of candidates did not exceed the number of available seats. When voting did take place, bribery and the provision of food and drink (treating) were often endemic. In the notoriously corrupt borough of Stafford, for instance, bribes of between £5 and £7 per vote were dispensed in the appropriately named "Tipping Street". Electioneering costs, not surprisingly, could be extremely high. Many a Victorian MP emptied the family coffers at the hands of unscrupulous agents and venal electorates. Standard costs ranged from around £1,000

political campaigns, most early 19th-century elections continued to be dominated by the personalities and influence of local, mainly landed, elites. Their rivalries and the mustering of their supporters under local campaign colours set the tone and agenda for polls that were almost feudal trials of strength. This was especially true in the county constituencies, where the votes cast, in the words of one seasoned election agent, resembled "a topography of the great estates". Deference to landlords and employers, shared economic interests and local religious identities further underpinned the community-based nature of early 19th-century elections. When national issues featured at all, they were usually viewed through a distinctly local lens.

The move towards a more recognisably modern electoral system, oriented around nationally organised parties, owed much to the gradual extension of voting rights under the three Reform Acts of 1832, 1867 and 1884. As electorates expanded, older forms of electioneering based on personal contact with each elector became impractical. Instead, candidates became ever more reliant on national party appeals and the work of party associations to attract and mobilise support. At the same time bribery and treating not only became more expensive, but also subject to far stricter control, though it would take the anonymity of the secret ballot and the curbs on expenses of the 1883 Corrupt Practices Act to limit such practices effectively.

Expanding electorates, however, were not the only force changing elections in the 19th century. As late as 1857, one-fifth of voters in English double-member seats were still "splitting" their two votes between candidates from opposite parties. This cross-party voting, supported by local traditions of independence and by open polling, acted as an important brake on the development of modern electoral partisanship. "In every constituency there are many voters who, from various motives, desire to please both parties, and therefore divide their votes," observed an 1868 election manual.

Secret voting after 1872 released electors from the pressures of public scrutiny and local influence, accelerating the development of an electoral culture based around individual party allegiances and the party platform. However, it was the replacement of double-member constituencies with single-member districts—leaving voters with only one vote to cast

—which ultimately forced every voter to make a choice for one party or another. By 1900, much of the public spectacle and community activity associated with open voting had been replaced by the sober solitude of a curtained poll booth.

Parliament and state regulation in the 19th century

The 19th century is often characterised as an era of minimal central government, free trade and *laissez-faire*. According to this view, the British state was smaller and interfered less in the lives of its subjects than it had done in the 18th century, when it had been geared to waging a series of intercontinental wars against France, or in the 20th century, when the state began to provide an increasing range of public services. Social critics such as the Victorian novelist Charles Dickens, setting the tone for later commentators, complained that social evils, such as poverty, disease and ignorance, flourished in the absence of state regulation and action.

Such a view, however, ignores the wide range of public services and social provision that was funded and delivered locally. It also ignores the fact that throughout the century there was a gradual expansion of infrastructure, regulation and social policy, to give just a few examples, all of which involved the state. In both of these aspects, parliament played a crucial role.

While the central state bureaucracy, or "Whitehall" as it is termed today, was small, this was only possible because many functions were delivered and administered by local bodies with powers to raise rates (local property taxes) to provide services. After 1834, the system of English public welfare, the poor law, was financed and distributed through locally elected bodies called boards of guardians. Locally elected highway commissions raised rates for the maintenance of roads, while improvement commissions served a similar purpose for paving and lighting many towns. After the reform of local government in 1835, elected town councils began to take on many of the functions that had previously been exercised by these separate bodies. After 1870, locally elected school boards had the responsibility of overseeing educational provision and funding it through local rates.

All of these local bodies derived their powers from legislation passed by parliament. In the early 19th century, many localities lobbied parliament for Local Acts to enable them to establish

Above: The terrace of the Palace of Westminster, 1909, by Emily Maria (Molly) Childers

individual highway or improvement commissions. General or public legislation, such as the 1834 Poor Law Amendment Act or the 1870 Elementary Education Act, required the creation of local bodies across the whole country. By the middle of the century there was a relative decline of Local Acts (which were expensive to secure) in favour of general legislation, enabling, but not forcing, local government to take on new functions. For example, the 1848 Public Health Act enabled town councils to establish local boards of health, but did not compel them to do so.

Such "permissive" legislation was favoured because the Victorian public and politicians were sensitive about "centralisation". The memory of the "warfare" state of the 18th century and comparisons with the authoritarian states of continental Europe meant that liberals and radicals in particular were wary of an over-mighty state which would threaten local and individual liberties. Permissive legislation seemed to strike a convenient balance between encouraging local initiatives to respond to social and urban problems, while safeguarding local independence from

Gladstone and Disraeli

The rivalry between William Gladstone and Benjamin Disraeli is the most famous duel in modern British political history. In their long careers they each served as chancellor of the exchequer and as prime minister (Gladstone as a Liberal in 1868–74, 1880–85, 1886, 1892–94, Disraeli for the Conservatives in 1868, 1874–80), and confronted one another in the Commons as leaders of their parties for more than 10 years. However, the personal and political antagonism between them has been exaggerated. In the 1830s, both were Tories and shared a similar political ideology, and they remained potential allies rather than enemies until the late 1850s. However, the two had radically different personalities and backgrounds. Gladstone represented urban interests associated with northern England and leaned towards evangelicalism, while Disraeli was Jewish by birth, but had converted to Anglicanism, and championed the agricultural interests of the Home Counties.

Inevitably these distinctions engendered mutual misunderstanding and mistrust—Gladstone disapproved of Disraeli's flippancy, opportunism and personal ambition, while the latter disliked his rival's arrogance and sanctimonious lack of humour. Nevertheless, while both men remained wary of each other's political intentions, each admired the other's remarkable personal gifts and political talents. As rival party leaders in the 1860s and 1870s they frequently clashed in the Commons, but neither was typical of his respective party, and each was amenable to compromise on important national questions. However, their dealings did become embittered in the mid-1870s, largely over questions of foreign policy. Although the personal rancour was short-lived, and Disraeli's move to the Lords in 1876 (as the Earl of Beaconsfield) ended their clashes in the Commons, Gladstone continued to publicly attack his rival's policies until Disraeli's death in 1881.

Caricatures of Gladstone at the despatch box (opposite) by the Victorian and Edwardian cartoonist Harry Furniss. A cartoon from Punch of March 1868 (above), with Disraeli (left), weeks after he had become prime minister, and Gladstone, who would form his first ministry after the election later that year

"While Victorian parliamentarians had a general preference to avoid intervention, this did not stop them passing pioneering legislation to protect workers, consumers and the environment"

central interference. When central bodies such as the Poor Law Commission were created to oversee and ensure some uniformity across local bodies, they were often very unpopular. Men at the commission, founded in the 1830s, were dubbed the "tyrants of Somerset House", in reference to their London headquarters.

Moreover, the state and parliament played a key part in economic development, the growth of social policy and industrial regulation. As the building of new roads, canals or docks in the 18th century had done, the construction of railway lines required the sanction of legislation, as did the continuing enclosure of land. Thus parliament was key to the reshaping of the British landscape in the 19th century through private legislation secured by railway companies and landowners.

The state's role in intervention and regulation in the early industrial economy in order to protect workers and consumers was more controversial. Early in the century, many industrialists and political economists argued in and outside parliament that the state's role in the economy should be limited to upholding contracts and property rights and dismantling barriers to trade. These issues aroused lively debates in parliament, which resulted in the gradual expansion of state activity in this area.

There was a familiar pattern to such developments. A good example is the passage of the Factory Acts to regulate child labour in the 1830s and 1840s. The harsh working conditions experienced by children working in Lancashire's cotton industry attracted increasing public and media attention by the 1830s. Humanitarian campaigners, including MPs like Lord Ashley (later the Earl of Shaftesbury) and Michael Sadler, called for the state to regulate conditions and limit working hours for women and

children. There was a series of parliamentary inquiries and bills promoted by individual members, until the Whig government passed the 1833 Factory Act. This limited hours and established an inspectorate to enforce the legislation. Criticised as inadequate, the measure was subsequently strengthened by acts passed in 1844, 1847 and 1850, which closed loopholes and reduced the working day in cotton factories to 10 hours.

Legislation to protect consumers from adulterated food and drink followed a similar path. A permissive bill was passed in 1858 after parliamentary inquiries. This enabled local government to appoint scientists to check for adulteration, and allowed councils to impose fines. It was further reinforced by legislation passed in the 1870s. The Victorian parliament was also the first to pass laws in response to the air pollution produced by the Industrial Revolution.

While Victorian parliamentarians generally preferred to avoid intervention this did not stop them passing pioneering legislation to protect workers, consumers and the environment. Much of it operated at a local level, with the laws evolving in a piecemeal, case-by-case way. Nevertheless, it set important precedents that were built on by the 20th-century state.

The Irish question

Irish representation under the Act of Union of 1801 was based on the country's wealth, rather than its population. This, and the government's failure to enable Catholics to sit in parliament—despite the fact that they had been able to vote in parliamentary elections since 1793—deprived the Union of widespread popular support. Opposition was first organised by the Catholic Committee in 1804. By 1823, the movement had embraced wider political aims under the energetic leadership of Daniel O'Connell.

By looking beyond Catholic emancipation to the repeal of the Union and the restoration of an Irish parliament equal in status to that of Great Britain, O'Connell skilfully exploited popular resentment against a settlement that increasingly appeared

Luke Hansard (1756– 1833), the founder of the Hansard dynasty, father of Thomas Curson Hansard, by Samuel Lane

Hansard

The official published reports of parliamentary debates in Britain (and also in some Commonwealth countries) are customarily referred to as *Hansard*, taking their name from the printer and publisher Thomas Curson Hansard (1776–1833). In 1812, Hansard took over the publication of parliamentary debates from the radical journalist William Cobbett, who had been producing them since 1803. Like Cobbett, Hansard compiled his accounts of parliamentary proceedings from newspaper reports, particularly *The Times*. Although *Hansard* eventually dominated, it was not the only such publication in the early 19th century. Its most notable rival, the *Mirror of Parliament*, which ran from 1828 until 1841, included the youthful Charles Dickens among its reporters.

Although it was still technically a breach of parliamentary privilege (until 1971) to publish reports of debates, the 19th century saw a growing acceptance of the importance of parliament's deliberations being

disseminated to the public. In 1803, the Commons Speaker arranged for the reporters to have special access to the gallery, and a separate reporters' gallery was provided both in the temporary House of Commons erected after the 1834 fire at Westminster, and in the new House designed by Sir Charles Barry.

From 1877, Thomas Curson Hansard junior (1813–91), who had succeeded his father, received an annual subsidy for the publication, on condition that he included reports of debates on private bills and in committee, as well as debates after midnight, which the newspapers tended to neglect. He therefore had to employ his own reporters for this purpose. Following problems with a series of private printers from 1889, parliament took over the publication of debates in 1909, with its own reporting staff, finally giving the publication official status. It temporarily dropped the name *Hansard*, but this remained in common usage, and was reinstated in 1943.

to operate to Ireland's disadvantage. His election to
the Commons in 1828 as MP for Clare, for which
he was as a Catholic not qualified to sit, led directly
to the Catholic Emancipation Act (or Roman
Catholic Relief Act) of 1829. Catholics were no longer
prevented from sitting in parliament because of their
religion—but the act severely reduced the size of the
Irish electorate by raising the property qualification
in the counties.

The Irish Reform Act of 1832, however, partly
compensated for the 1829 change. It increased the
country's representation from 100 to 105 MPs and
increased the electorate by one quarter. It ushered in
a period of cooperation between O'Connell and the
Whig governments of the 1830s, which resulted in
reforms to systems of town government, education
and church funding, and the introduction of an Irish
poor law. Yet the Union would remain problematic
while a Protestant minority continued to monopolise
Ireland's administrative and judicial offices. In spite of
being plentifully supplied with information about the
country, the Westminster parliament frequently failed
to act promptly or intelligently to overcome Ireland's
problems. Many of these arose from the land tenure
system, and the fact that in much of the country the
land was owned by Protestants of English origin but
farmed by an Irish Catholic peasantry.

Although popular support for repeal of the
Union grew after 1840, O'Connell's movement made
little impact on political arrangements between Great
Britain and Ireland before becoming hopelessly
divided in 1847. By then, the catastrophic failure
of the potato crop due to disease and the resultant
widespread famine and depopulation of the country
had prompted opponents of the Union to more
radical action. An abortive rebellion in 1848 soon
gave way to more measured attempts to secure rights
for farm tenants and establish an independent Irish
party at Westminster. Although these campaigns
were aided by a considerable increase in Ireland's

*Right: The Home Rule Debate
in the House of Lords 1893, by
Dickinson Foster. The Marquess
of Salisbury is standing at the
despatch box, speaking against
the bill, which the Lords rejected
in a blow to Gladstone's attempt
to settle "The Irish question"*

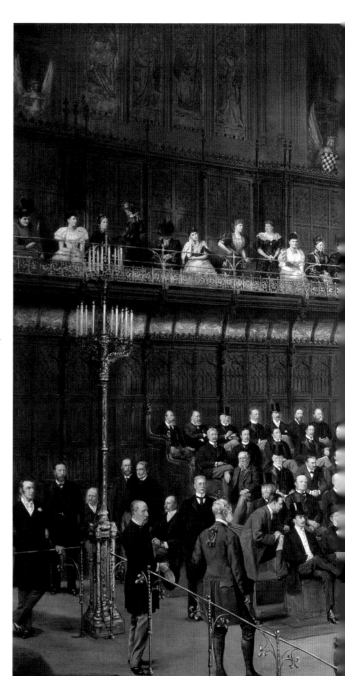

"The catastrophic failure of the potato crop due to disease prompted opponents of the Union to more radical action"

county electorate under the 1850 Franchise Act, they failed to achieve their main objectives. By the 1860s, the aims of the Union's opponents tended towards separatism, relying if necessary on violence. Unlike O'Connell, the radical Fenian movement sought to establish an independent Irish republic, rather than a self-governing colony within the empire.

The Second Reform Act had little impact in Ireland, but the abject failure of the Fenian rising in 1867 diverted political dissent back towards constitutional reform, beginning in 1869 with the disestablishment of the (Anglican) Irish Church, an institution that had once been seen as an essential pillar of the Union. The home rule movement led by Isaac Butt in the 1870s promoted federal devolution, with a subordinate Dublin Parliament dealing with Irish affairs alone. Under the more effective leadership of Charles Stewart Parnell, who forged a powerful alliance of Irish parliamentarians, land reformers and Irish-American republicans, the home rule party developed the capacity to paralyse the legislative process at Westminster. The great expansion of the Irish electorate in 1884–85 and the adoption of single member constituencies under the Third Reform Act greatly increased Parnell's parliamentary following and persuaded prime minister William Gladstone of the case for home rule.

Gladstone's 1886 home rule bill, which envisaged a single chamber legislature for Ireland with largely local powers, was defeated in the Commons. A second bill in 1893, which proposed an elected bicameral parliament, was rejected by the Lords. Nevertheless, Irish influence at Westminster did help to secure a transformation of the land system between 1870 and 1903. The campaign was characterised by bitter and violent struggle and tempered by timely concessions from successive Liberal and Unionist governments. It effectively subverted the political and administrative ascendancy of the country's landed elite and thus removed another buttress of the Union.

In 1912, what was now called the Irish Nationalist party secured a third home rule bill from the Liberal government. It was passed by the Commons but delayed by the Lords. Opposition to the measure in Protestant-dominated regions of Ulster briefly raised the prospect of civil conflict but tensions dissipated at the outbreak of the First World War in August 1914. Nevertheless, the heavy-handed suppression of the republicans' 1916 Easter Rising in Dublin destroyed hopes for a constitutional settlement of the home rule question. It sparked an insurgency that only came to an end in December 1921 with the conclusion of the Anglo-Irish Treaty. The Government of Ireland Act subsequently established a 26-county Irish Free State, a self-governing dominion, independent, but still in the empire. The remaining six counties of Ulster became Northern Ireland, with its own parliament, but still part of the United Kingdom.

This solution had only limited success. In the south a civil war was followed by a prolonged period of political friction between the Dublin and London governments before an Irish republic was established in 1949. Twenty years later, the unresolved consequences of partition brought about the "troubles" in Northern Ireland, where a Unionist majority had monopolised government since 1920 and a nationalist minority largely repudiated an authority it could not hope to wield. A civil rights campaign, which ended in violence, ushered in 30 years of political and sectarian conflict before a peace process was established in 1998.

Votes for women

In 1866, the Liberal MP John Stuart Mill presented a petition to the House of Commons asking for the elective franchise to be extended to all householders "without distinction of sex". The petition had 1,521 signatures. Although the history of women and the vote goes back before this, the 1866 petition—organised by the Women's Suffrage Petition Committee, led by Barbara Bodichon—marked the beginning of organised campaigning and lobbying of parliament by a variety of national and local women's suffrage societies. Nearly 12,000 petitions for women's

"The Home-Rulers stood up, and for some time, with raised hands, shouted 'Privilege!'"—*Times*, Feb. 3.

Left: Members of the Irish party demonstrate in the Commons Chamber in February 1881 against the Irish Coercion bill. One of them, Michael Davitt (inset), was currently in prison

Charles Stewart Parnell, caricature by "T", 1880

Parnell and obstruction

Although Charles Stewart Parnell (1846–91) came from the Protestant landholding class, he became a surprising recruit to the cause of Irish home rule and land reform. An MP from 1875, from the 1877 session of parliament he brilliantly developed an old parliamentary weapon. This was the practice of obstruction —preventing progress on bills by continuing debate on them for as long as possible, thus wrecking the plans of government for legislation. The campaign reached its height in the opposition to the Irish Coercion Bill in early 1881. The bill was a response to the sometimes violent confrontations in Ireland between landlords and tenants, stimulated by the Fenian movement. It allowed for imprisonment without trial for those linked to the agitation. Parnell, newly elected to the leadership of the Irish Parliamentary Party at Westminster, orchestrated a campaign of obstruction that kept the House sitting for two days—41 hours —before it was brought to an end by the Speaker, Sir Henry Brand, acting on his own authority. The incident helped to bring about a series of procedural innovations that would eventually limit the ability of individual MPs to oppose the will of the majority of the House.

Parnell tried to build alliances between the parliamentary party and, on the one hand, the radical and republican Fenian movement and on the other the Liberal party under Gladstone. While unionists tried to destroy him with forged evidence of his support for the murder of the chief British minister for Ireland in Dublin in 1882, the more radical end of the Irish nationalist movement increasingly saw him as much too conservative for their purposes. His leadership of the party was destroyed when a former Irish MP, the husband of his long-standing mistress, Kitty O'Shea, filed for divorce, to the outrage of most nationalists and many within the Liberal party.

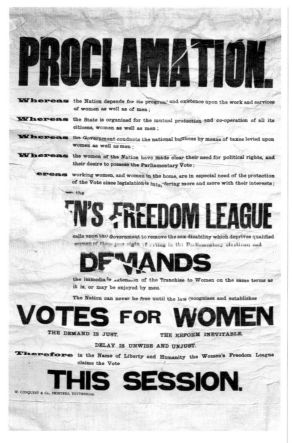

PROCLAMATION.

Whereas the Nation depends for its progress and existence upon the work and services of women as well as of men;

Whereas the State is organised for the mutual protection and co-operation of all its citizens, women as well as men;

Whereas the Government conducts the national business by means of taxes levied upon women as well as men;

Whereas the women of the Nation have made clear their need for political rights, and their desire to possess the Parliamentary Vote;

Whereas working women, and women in the home, are in especial need of the protection of the Vote since legislation is interfering more and more with their interests;

the **WOMEN'S FREEDOM LEAGUE**

calls upon the Government to remove the sex disability which deprives qualified women of their just right of voting in the Parliamentary elections and

DEMANDS

the immediate extension of the Franchise to Women on the same terms as it is, or may be enjoyed by men.

The Nation can never be free until the law recognises and establishes

VOTES FOR WOMEN

THE DEMAND IS JUST.   THE REFORM INEVITABLE.

DELAY IS UNWISE AND UNJUST.

Therefore in the Name of Liberty and Humanity the Women's Freedom League claims the Vote

THIS SESSION.

W. CONQUEST & Co., PRINTERS, TOTTENHAM.

suffrage were presented to the Commons between 1866 and 1918, and hundreds more to the Lords.

The first full parliamentary debate on the subject took place in 1867 with Mill's unsuccessful attempt to amend the Second Reform Bill to substitute the word "man" with "person". It continued with bills or motions being presented to the Commons by individual MPs almost every year between 1870 and 1914, resulting in many debates and votes on the subject. Sometimes supporters of women's suffrage even won a vote. No government, however, was prepared to introduce its own bill or to help an individual MP to get his bill through parliament. Without that support, all of this effort was in vain.

In 1897, a number of local societies formed the National Union of Women's Suffrage Societies (NUWSS) under the leadership of Millicent Garrett Fawcett. The NUWSS and its member societies pursued constitutional means of political campaigning such as petitioning, lobbying, deputations, meetings, and peaceful rallies and marching. Its supporters were known as "suffragists". Some women were impatient with the lack of progress by suffragists, and in 1903 the Women's Social and Political Union (WSPU) was founded by Emmeline Pankhurst and others. The WSPU's motto, "Deeds Not Words", encapsulated their different approach. Their methods of direct action, which began in late 1905 and developed and escalated over time, took many forms, including setting fire to pillar boxes, stone-throwing and window-breaking. Supporters of the WSPU and other militant organisations became known as "suffragettes". The Palace of Westminster was a particular target for suffragettes. Well-known incidents included the "rush" on the building organised by the WSPU in June 1908; the chaining of suffragettes from the Women's Freedom League to the grilles of the Ladies' Gallery in October 1908; and Emily Wilding Davison's overnight stay in the Chapel of St Mary Undercroft on census night 1911.

In 1909, Marion Wallace-Dunlop was the first suffragette to go on hunger strike, following imprisonment for stencilling a notice on a wall in St Stephen's Hall. Initially hunger-striking women were released. Later the tactic of forcible feeding was adopted. This barbaric method caused revulsion and an outcry. Politicians including the Labour Party founder Keir Hardie spoke out in parliament against it, and George Lansbury resigned his seat to fight a by-election on the issue, unsuccessfully. To overcome the protests the Prisoners (Temporary Discharge for Ill-health) Act was passed in 1913, which allowed for hunger-striking prisoners to be released until they regained their health—at which point they were then re-arrested. This was likened by campaigners to a cat playing with a mouse, and the legislation became better known as "the Cat and Mouse Act".

At the outbreak of the First World War, all suffragette prisoners were released, militancy ended

Right: Suffragette "General" Mrs Drummond in a boat opposite the terrace of the House of Commons, 1908, inviting MPs to a demonstration in Hyde Park

and active campaigning was suspended, although it carried on behind the scenes. Suffrage campaigners were divided in their attitude to the war, with some supportive and others against. Many women mobilised in support of the war effort to free men for active service, taking over traditionally male jobs in factories, offices, transport, agriculture, and munitions work, to much press and public acclaim.

The war necessitated electoral reform, primarily to ensure all returning soldiers could vote and would not be disqualified by property or residential requirements. A conference, chaired by the Speaker of the House of Commons, was held during 1916–17 to discuss the extent of reform required. The resulting Representation of the People Act 1918 gave the vote in parliamentary elections to all men over the age of 21, and women over the age of 30 who met minimum property qualifications. Nearly 13 million men and eight and a half million women were now eligible to vote. The age restriction was designed to ensure women did not form the majority of the electorate, as they would otherwise have done because of the loss of men in the war. It took a further 10 years of bills, parliamentary debate and campaigning by women's organisations before Baldwin's Conservative government passed the Equal Franchise Act 1928. This gave women the vote on the same terms as men, at age 21.

A separate act, the Parliament (Qualification of Women) Act 1918, allowed women to stand for election to the House of Commons. The first to be elected was Constance Markievicz in 1918, though, as a member of Sinn Fein, demanding Irish independence, she did not take her seat. She was followed in 1919 by Nancy Astor, the first woman to take her seat. Women were allowed to sit in the House of Lords as life peers following the Life Peerages Act 1958. Five years later, the Peerage Act 1963 allowed hereditary women peers to sit, and full parliamentary equality was finally reached. However, the number of women members has grown only slowly over time, and even today, women make up less than a quarter of the membership in both Houses of Parliament.

Exporting parliament

In the 19th century, Britain acquired the largest empire in history. The dilemma facing British policy makers was whether

to maintain imperial rule by exerting executive control from London or to allow greater colonial self-government.

By the 1830s, the Empire extended to Australia, India, South Africa, the West Indies and British North America. With the task of governing such a diverse range of colonies becoming increasingly complex and expensive, the British government began to accept that greater self-government was necessary. The belief that British institutions were superior was entrenched in the thinking of ministers and civil servants in its Colonial Office. Therefore their preferred solution was to export the "Westminster model" of government. In theory, this meant establishing a constitution where the ruling government was made up of ministers drawn from an elected legislature. This was known as representative or "responsible" government.

In reality, however, it was difficult to reproduce the Westminster system in colonies that had fundamentally different societies to Britain. While representative self-government could be deemed suitable for white settler colonies such as British North America, British policymakers feared that it would be unworkable in colonial societies dominated by indigenous peoples, such as Trinidad or Ceylon (present-day Sri Lanka). The subsequent extension of greater representative self-government throughout the British Empire was therefore haphazard.

Even in the white settler colonies, the process of establishing Westminster-style parliaments was not always completely straightforward. Following a rebellion in Lower Canada in 1837, Lord Durham, sent by the government to investigate the crisis, recommended the union of Upper and Lower Canada, along with the introduction of responsible government.

"Beginning in 1855, the Australian colonies were given self-government along the lines of the Westminster model, whereby the parliaments consisted of two chambers"

The 1840 Act of Union united the two provinces and created a single legislature, though the Governor-General, appointed by the British government, remained an interventionist figure, weakening analogies with the Westminster parliament.

British colonial governors, answerable to the home parliament, were also dominant figures in Australian colonies in the first half of the 19th century. This was especially the case in New South Wales, where British officials felt that a former convict society was not politically mature enough to benefit from greater participation in government. The escalating cost and inconvenience of controlling a colony so far away from London, however, soon proved too much.

Beginning in 1855, the Australian colonies were given self-government along the lines of the Westminster model, whereby their parliaments consisted of two chambers, an Assembly and a Council, the former being elected on a wide male franchise. The architecture of these parliaments also reflected British influences. The design of Parliament House in Adelaide, South Australia, for example, built in 1889, was modelled on the Victorian neoclassical style of Leeds Town Hall. Inside the Australian state assemblies, members of the government and the opposition were seated on opposite sides of the debating chamber, echoing the arrangement of the House of Commons, although a clear two-party system did not emerge until the early 20th century.

In 1901, the six separate colonies joined to form the Commonwealth of Australia, with both men and women over the age of 21 able to vote in federal elections. The first British colony to grant women the right to vote in parliamentary elections was New Zealand in 1893, 25 years before the enfranchisement of women in Britain.

In contrast to Australia and New Zealand, colonies dominated by races other than white Europeans were definitely not deemed ready for responsible government. Successive British ministries were keen to maintain autocratic rule to keep potential social problems in check. In Cape Colony, for example, the prevalence of racial tensions and the importance of maintaining the territory for military defence delayed the introduction of greater self-government until the 1870s.

Racial conflict was also present in Jamaica, a British colony that had its own ancient system of representative government. In 1866, the predominantly white Jamaican Assembly, terrified by the continuing rise in black political power, readily accepted direct rule from Britain. The assembly was replaced by a half-nominated, half-elected Legislative Council, dominated by the British-appointed governor, Edward Eyre, who disingenuously lamented the loss of "institutions so deservedly dear to every British heart".

The extent to which representative self-government was exported throughout the British Empire was therefore determined by the nature of the individual territories, and even in white settler colonies, it was often impractical to create an exact replica of the Westminster model, with its lower and upper chambers. The form of a local elected legislature was always adapted to meet the particular conditions of a colony.

Opposite: Nancy Astor, Viscountess Astor, campaigning in the Plymouth by-election in 1919. She won and became the first woman to take her seat in the House of Commons

Chapter six—
Parliament in modern times

The widening of the electorate was a challenge for a country that celebrated the antiquity and strength of its parliamentary tradition. Democracy produced some stresses and strains as governments determined to reshape the state sometimes found themselves frustrated by the formalities and delays of parliamentary procedure. Political parties fighting elections on a national basis needed to exert stronger discipline over their MPs, a process that could lead to disillusionment and disengagement among the electorate. Parliament itself could seem remote to many electors, its reputation tarnished by a series of scandals. Yet in some ways parliament has become more effective, providing more detailed scrutiny of government policies and decisions than ever before.

Contributors—
Mark Collins
Paul Seaward

The election of 1918 would mark a watershed in British political life. Gone were a large number of the Irish MPs—the Sinn Fein members seceded to form their own parliament, the Dail, in Dublin and three years later, the Anglo-Irish Treaty meant the loss of all of the members from territory of the new Irish Free State. The changes of 1918 and 1928 to the franchise, including the enfranchisement of women, dramatically increased the electorate, to more than 21 million in 1919, and nearly 29 million in 1929 (out of a total population of around 45 million).

One result of the expansion of the mandate was the rapid increase in the vote gained by the young Labour party. Though their 63 seats in the 1918 election made up less than 10 per cent of the number of seats in the House, by 1922 they were the second largest party with 142 seats. In 1923, they obtained sufficient seats to form a government—although only for a brief period in a situation in which no party had an absolute majority. In 1929, they did become the largest party for the first time, although again they had no absolute majority and again the government of the first Labour prime minister, Ramsay Macdonald, collapsed under the pressure of a worldwide economic crisis soon afterwards. It was their highest point for a long time.

Many of the party's gains since 1918 were reversed in the election of 1931, and the party split when Macdonald agreed to join the Conservatives in a coalition—the National Government—to take the steps necessary to deal with the crisis. It took time for the Labour party to rebuild its strength and patch over divisions to which the Labour movement was always prone. Yet the Liberal party had suffered badly since the First World War as well. It had split in 1918

over the continuation of its wartime coalition with the Conservatives under the premiership of David Lloyd George. There had been a catastrophic decline in its own vote. Its acceptance of a fresh coalition in the 1931 crisis very nearly spelt the end of its existence as a viable party.

These splits between the First and Second World Wars were partly the reason why each party made a greater effort to ensure that its MPs stuck to the agreed party line. One way of doing so was to create structures so that the leadership could keep in close touch with the "backbenchers"—a relatively new term for those who did not hold positions as ministers. (The term "shadow ministers", the team of the official spokesmen for the opposition whose job was to respond to the government's policies and statements was used after 1945 as the opposition became more formalised.) A backbench revolt against the Conservative party leadership finally ended the Liberal–Conservative coalition in 1922. After the election later that year, new Conservative MPs formed the "1922 Committee", which would become a forum for all Conservative backbenchers. Ever since it became a significant group at the 1906 election the Labour party had held regular meetings of all of its (far fewer) MPs, known as the Parliamentary Labour Party, or PLP.

The political effects of the growing working class vote had already been apparent before 1918. The landslide Liberal election victory of 1906 had brought to power a government with a radical programme of reform influenced by its pact with the early Labour party. One key change was the introduction of payments for MPs (though one that the government was reluctant to describe as a "salary" because of conservative opposition to the idea that MPs would become some sort of

Right: The 29 Labour MPs elected in 1906 photographed on the terrace of the House of Commons. Their chairman and leader, Keir Hardie, is in the centre. Ramsay Macdonald, who would become the first Labour prime minister, is the second on Hardie's right

"The reduction in the powers of the Lords to resist government legislation had made it easier for a radical reforming government to bring about change"

Right: One of the first non-white Members of Parliament, Sir Mancherjee Merwanjee Bhownagree (1851–1933) was elected in 1895 and 1906 for the North London constituency of Bethnal Green as a Unionist (Conservative)

Opposite: Typists and reporters producing the report of debates for one of the new standing committees in a photograph from 1919

government official). This made it possible for working men —for whom it was exceptionally difficult to finance a political career—to serve as MPs.

The 1906 Liberal government's large majority meant that it had little effective opposition in the Commons. But the House of Lords, dominated by Conservatives, had acted as a block on the Irish home rule plans of a previous Liberal government. Now it blocked the new government's education reforms and the 1909 "People's Budget", devised by the dynamic and determined chancellor of the exchequer, David Lloyd George, to help fund a series of welfare reforms.

A confrontation between the two Houses brought about two elections in the course of 1910.

The result was an Act of Parliament that permanently reduced the powers of the House of Lords. The Parliament Act of 1911 ensured that the Lords would never again be able to block government legislation altogether, but only delay it for up to two years. But it left the question of the membership of the House of Lords unresolved. Still made up of men who had inherited their right to sit in parliament, it had long seemed out of date. Revelations that peerages had gone to businessmen in return for donations to party funds, particularly associated with Lloyd George when he was premier, tainted the House, and politics, with a whiff of sleaze as well. But uncertain about how to replace the present system, politicians decided to leave the question for another day.

The reduction in the powers of the Lords to resist government legislation had made it easier for a radical reforming government to bring about change—though some thought it was still not enough. It had become easier for governments to get bills through the Commons too. In the course of the 19th century, the government had already managed to get the Commons to agree that it should have the right to decide the agenda—to have the "legislative initiative"—for most of the time the House was sitting. But the very effective campaign of "obstruction" by the Irish party in the 1880s, and the increasing pressure of MPs to raise issues on the floor of the House made further changes necessary if the government was going to be able to get bills passed into law.

In the 1880s, both Liberal and Conservative governments had managed to persuade the House

to accept new rules which meant that a majority of members could prevent further discussion on any subject and to force a vote. The "guillotine" and "closure" then introduced limited the opportunities for "filibustering"—the practice of speaking for hours on a motion in order to prevent it from ever being decided. The House established a new system of "standing committees" to consider the detail of bills, freeing time on the floor of the House for new business. New rules brought in during the 1890s and 1900s made the process of getting the government's financial plans (the "estimates") approved much more straightforward.

These changes made the House of Commons much more efficient at processing legislation.

But they encouraged fears that parliament was becoming dominated by government. They were coupled with the increasing willingness of MPs, more conscious than ever before that they had been elected as part of a national effort by their party, to vote the way their party leadership told them to. The two world wars of 1914–18 and 1939–45 exacerbated the problem: no general elections were held during either conflict, some parliamentary sessions were held in secret, and legislation was hurried through because of the emergency. Some of it, like the Defence of the Realm Act, passed in 1914, and the Emergency Powers (Defence) Act of 1940, provided the government with very extensive powers. The executive, many

Above: Crowds outside the Houses of Parliament in 1939 waiting for a statement by prime minister Neville Chamberlain on war with Germany

felt, was now able to tell the legislature just what to do, although it was not until the 1960s that Quintin Hogg, Lord Hailsham, popularised the term "elective dictatorship".

Yet parliament's presence throughout the wars, sitting throughout the Blitz and the Battle of Britain in the thick of the battle in central London, seemed also to show the strength of the tradition of representative government. Moreover, the dangers of domination by the executive were of course vastly different from the problems faced by the citizens of many other European states during the 1920s and 1930s—in Spain, Italy, and Germany—where quite recently created parliaments were either abolished or turned into puppet assemblies. The feeling that Britain was one of a diminishing number

of parliamentary and democratic states gave a sense that it was vital to protect the quality of its political life and institutions. That sense was powerful during the Second World War, when the Palace of Westminster itself was bombed during the Blitz, and helped to make parliament's standing in the eyes of the public as high as at any time before.

Cradle to grave: legislating and the boundaries of the state

The amount and range of legislation passed by parliament has been growing since the 18th century. But the period since 1906, and particularly since 1945, has seen a huge expansion in parliament's workload. In the 19th century, parliament would pass legislation that enabled bodies such as local authorities to take up the regulation of economic activity in their own areas. The 20th century saw a massive growth in the determination of central government not just to enable others to regulate the

Sir Winston Churchill visiting the bombed-out chamber of the House of Commons

The bombing of the Palace of Westminster, 1941

The night of Saturday 10 May and Sunday 11 May 1941 was said to be the worst night of the London Blitz. The Palace of Westminster had been hit several times before, but on this occasion there was serious damage in seven different areas. Fires were started by incendiary bombs. The Clock Tower was struck, but the clock ("Big Ben") kept working. Three people were killed.

With the roof of Westminster Hall already alight, and the Victorian Commons' chamber ablaze; it was decided that the "sham" Gothic of the chamber should be let go in favour of the great medieval masterpiece—the Hall roof. By the end of the night, the oak timbers of the hall had been doused with water and saved. Westminster Hall was one of the most important sites in the history of parliament, but the chamber was lost in which the words of Gladstone and Disraeli were heard, as well as the first speeches to the House as prime minister by Winston Churchill, such as that of 13 May 1940: "I have nothing to offer but blood, toil, tears and sweat ... Victory at all costs." The MPs moved to the House of Lords chamber. The Lords met in the Robing Room—another part of the Palace complex—until the end of the war. Many items were made from stone and lead debris salvaged from the ruins, which were sold after being fashioned into a variety of gifts to help the British Red Cross and St John War Organisation.

"After the Second World War, the Labour government elected in 1945 passed a series of far-reaching reforms"

economy, but itself to take on responsibility for regulation, and for providing basic services such as healthcare and education. Government departments grew in number, in size and in the scope of their work.

The great Liberal government reforms in the period after 1906 began the process, with the creation of old age pensions, and a system of national insurance and labour exchanges. Even before the First World War the civil service considerably more than doubled. Both wars took things much further, spawning new departments and increasing centralisation.

After the Second World War, the Labour government elected in 1945 passed a series of far-reaching reforms, building on the review of welfare undertaken in the November 1942 Beveridge Report. The National Health Service Act, the National Insurance Act and the National Assistance Act, all passed in the 1945–50 parliament, were among the essential pieces of legislation that went into creating a system of "cradle to grave" support for all members of the population. In fact, the process had already begun under the coalition government, with the 1944 Education Act extending free education to secondary level. But the Labour party's nationalisation of key sectors of the economy, including the iron and steel industries, aircraft and shipbuilding, were the subject of major battles between the parties throughout the post-war period.

All of this growth in the activity directly managed by the central government was a challenge to parliament. It meant that every person in the country now dealt directly with the central state about many vital services, and when the system went wrong MPs' constituents would complain about it to them. MPs needed to ask more questions to ministers about those services, either in "Question Time" in the House of Commons itself, or through correspondence.

Opposite: As Minister for Health in the 1945 Labour government, Aneurin (Nye) Bevan (1897–1960) pushed through the creation of the National Health Service

Left, from top: By 1935 there were still only nine women MPs. Five of them, all Conservatives, were assembled for this photograph —Irene Ward, Thelma Cazalet, the Duchess of Atholl, Mavis Tate and Florence Horsbrugh; a petition about the cost of living is delivered to an MP outside the House of Commons, around 1935

Churchill and Attlee

Churchill and Attlee together in a photograph of the War Cabinet in 1941

Sir Winston Churchill (1874–1965) is still probably the most famous politician Britain has ever produced, with an astonishingly long and full career. In parliament almost continuously from 1900 until 1964, he began as a Unionist (Conservative) MP, moved to the Liberals in 1904 and returned to the Conservative party in 1924. He first served as a minister in 1905, was called to the premiership at the height of the crisis of the defeat of France by Germany in 1940, leading the country for five years to victory in Europe in 1945. He finally left office in 1955 after a second term as peacetime prime minister, his fame assured by his dynamic wartime leadership and his gifts as an inspiring speaker.

Clement Attlee (1883–1967) was a very different character to Churchill: uncharismatic, but quietly efficient, a deeply respected manager, rather than an inspirational figure. By standing at the head of a government that brought in a swathe of reforms establishing the welfare state he also has a claim to be one of the most significant of Britain's prime ministers. He was elected leader of the Labour Party in 1935, and in the wartime coalition he acted as Churchill's deputy, although he was overshadowed by other Labour politicians in charge of major departments, such as Herbert Morrison and Ernest Bevin. Labour's massive election victory of 1945 enabled it to realise the scheme for a national welfare state envisaged in the wartime Beveridge Report.

Although colleagues in the wartime coalition, Churchill and Attlee were opponents after the war. Churchill was leader of the opposition during the 1945–51 Labour governments led by Attlee, and Attlee was leader of the opposition during Churchill's last premiership in 1951–55. Their clashes were less spectacular than those of Gladstone and Disraeli, or Pitt and Fox, because Churchill spent less time in the House of Commons during this late period and because Attlee was no great orator. Prime Minister's Question Time, which would make such confrontations into a regular feature of British political life, only took something close to its modern form and importance in 1961. But with Churchill's strong hostility to socialism, and Attlee's modest air, they represented very clearly not only two very different sets of belief, but also two very different styles of politics.

This growth in the size of the state came in large part to define the difference between the two main political parties. Labour saw state provision of key services as a way of countering the effects of inequality and deprivation. Many within the Conservative party saw it as inefficient and affecting private enterprise. Conservative efforts to limit the growth of the state included privatisation of many state-owned utilities and industries, especially under the premiership of Margaret Thatcher (1979–90). Some government activities would be placed in agencies at "arm's length" from ministers, so politicians would have less chance to become directly involved. But that might mean as well that it was more difficult for MPs to get to the bottom of problems that affected their constituents.

Keeping pace with changes in attitudes in society would also be a preoccupation of parliament after 1945. It was often done without the direction of successive governments, which often preferred to leave questions of morality to be decided by a "free vote"—without the government advising members which way it believed they should vote. The Sexual Offences Act (1967) legalised homosexual acts in private, after a long public debate and an inquiry by an expert group, the Wolfenden committee. Changes to family law have followed, including recently changing the definition of marriage to include same-sex marriage. The Abortion Act, also passed in 1967 on the initiative of an individual MP (though with support from the government) legalised abortion in specific circumstances, though the subject remains very controversial.

Parliament since 1945

In the election held in July 1945 following the defeat of Germany in the Second World War, the Labour Party roared to power with a landslide victory and almost 400 seats in the Commons, toppling the wartime premier, Sir Winston Churchill, and providing a platform for plans created during the war for a huge expansion of the welfare state. The creation of the National Health Service was its most notable achievement, but the nationalisation of some major industries was highly controversial and closely fought through the Commons. In order to speed the legislation

Below: Crowds in Parliament Square, Westminster as members of the new government are driven to the House of Commons following the July 1945 election

achievement in public life. They brought some new blood into an institution that had become virtually irrelevant to the real politics of parliament. Many were former MPs, and as their numbers grew they made it into a more political body, though they included men and women—the first women life peers were created in the same year—who brought to the House expertise in fields outside politics. The House of Lords became better respected for the quality of its debates and its work scrutinising the work of government and the proposals for legislation that originated in the European Community. But, though there was a healthy transformation in the capacity of the House, the Lords remained an odd sort of legislative chamber, with a membership either by appointment or by inheritance.

It was Labour that was most keen on further change, especially because the hereditary peers tended to be Conservative. The party eyed the chamber as a potential obstruction to some of its legislative plans following the landslide victory of Tony Blair in 1997. It initiated the most determined discussions of the future of the House which culminated in the removal of most of the hereditary peers under the House of Lords Act 1999. It was more difficult to decide how to replace them. The 1999 act did not answer the major questions about whether all or part of the House should consist of elected members and whether and how its powers should change.

These issues remain unsettled, largely because of concerns that an elected House of Lords would compete for power with the elected Commons on a more equal footing, giving rise to regular conflicts between the two chambers. There have been other changes, though, including the replacement of the lord chancellor as its presiding officer with a new,

Above: Black Rod summons the Commons to hear the Queen's Speech at the opening of parliament in 1978

Opposite: Prime minister Margaret Thatcher and members of her government (Geoffrey Howe, Keith Joseph, John Nott and Norman Tebbit) wait to be summoned to the House of Lords to hear the Queen's Speech, November 1981

through, the government expanded the system of legislative committees so that more business was taken "upstairs" in committee rooms rather than on the floor of the House. Fears of more determined resistance from the House of Lords brought about a new Parliament Act in 1949 which reduced further the amount of time the Lords could delay legislation.

Further reform of the House of Lords was still on the agenda of some politicians, though not very high up. An important change was the 1958 Life Peerages Act, which created a new type of peer. Life peers were men and women who were given the right to sit in the Lords as a result of some major

"A declining sense of party identity and engagement has been an important factor in the declining turnout in general elections"

Above: The 1997 election finally saw a leap in the numbers of women elected, to a total of 120, about 18 per cent. Most of them were Labour MPs, photographed here with prime minister Tony Blair

elected, Lord Speaker, emphasising the way in which the House has asserted control of its own affairs.

Parties were perhaps at their strongest after the Second World War. Sometimes they were seen as too powerful, robbing individual MPs of their independent initiative, the whips of either party exercising a sinister hold over them. In fact, whips acted as the essential means of connecting the party leaderships with their MPs, warning leaders away from policies that would threaten serious party splits or rows. Parties, though, coalitions of people with only broadly similar views, could still be difficult to keep together. The Labour party when in power under the premiership of Harold Wilson in 1964–70

struggled with its close but difficult relationship with the broader Labour movement, the trades unions. In the late 1970s, Labour, again in power, became deeply split between its left and right wings, leading to its defeat in 1979 by the Conservatives under Margaret Thatcher, the breakaway of some of its most prominent figures on the right to form the Social Democratic Party (SDP), and 18 years out of power.

Both parties were deeply damaged by disagreement over whether or not to join the European Community, and how far (once the United Kingdom had joined in 1973) to go in the process of European integration. The Conservatives were worst affected by the rows, if only because they were in power during the key debates. Enoch Powell—the most eloquent, widely admired and divisive politician of his generation—left the party in 1974 as a result of the UK's entry. The most bitter debates came over the Maastricht Treaty of 1992, which contributed to the party's defeat at the 1997 election and the rise of alternative parties demanding an exit from what had now become the European Union. These internal party divisions over Europe helped to weaken party control at the end of the 1990s.

Another factor in the difficulties of the political parties has been the decline in mass membership. The number of individual Labour party members, for example, was said to have peaked at more than a million during the early 1950s; Conservatives were reported as having over three million. In 2014, the individual membership of both parties was much less than 200,000. A declining sense of party identity and engagement has been an important factor in the declining turnout in general elections, down to 65 per cent in 2010 from figures above 80 per cent in the 1950s.

Churchill speaking at the laying of a foundation stone for the new House of Commons, May 1948. Attlee is standing behind him

Post-war rebuilding and expansion

On the 28 October 1943 the House debated the proposal for a new chamber to replace the one destroyed by bombing in 1941. "We shape our buildings," said Churchill, "and afterwards our buildings shape us." The old chamber had favoured the two-party system, based on debate across the floor of the house. The architect Giles Gilbert Scott (1880–1960) built his chamber on exactly the same footprint as the old one; it was kept deliberately too small to accommodate all members so that smaller debates would keep their sense of intimacy.

A modernist design was also considered alongside a gothic one. Some said that the old style of the destroyed chamber was something to be left in the past, but gothic won the day, giving a sense of continuity in a rapidly changing world. Opened in October 1950, the total cost was £2 million. The new chamber, built at a time of great austerity after the war, benefited from gifts of money and materials from all the Commonwealth countries.

From the 1960s, buildings nearby were acquired for members' offices. In 2001, Portcullis House was opened to house 210 MPs, allowing all members to have a room of their own for the first time. Restaurants are on the ground floor and committee rooms on the first floor. Advanced services were designed to cut costs and CO_2 emissions; the air is cooled by water from aquifers. A rectangular atrium is covered by a glazed roof supported by wooden struts, and although larger in area than Westminster Hall, the new courtyard recalls its medieval neighbour.

Above: The Scottish parliament at Holyrood, in the new parliament building where it has met since 2004

Opposite: The Palace of Westminster, Westminster Bridge and the new building, Portcullis House, from across the river

Parties are not, either, quite so much the focus of each MPs' attention while in parliament as they once were. One of the major reasons for this is the growth of the select committee system. The select committees that are well known today grew out of a series of previous systems created for scrutinising the government's financial estimates, which the House itself had long abandoned looking at in detail. Such committees were disliked by governments, which saw them as likely to interfere in the detail of administration and the responsibility of ministers themselves. Yet it was widely felt that parliament needed some mechanism by which it could look much more closely at the work of central government, now vastly grown in size since the 19th century.

In 1979, the new government of Margaret Thatcher accepted a proposal made by a committee of MPs in the previous parliament. It established a structure of "select" committees that shadowed the various government departments. The new structure has grown into one of the most important parts of parliamentary activity. Committees have become much better staffed since their early days, and the job of chairman of each committee has become recognised as a very significant role within parliament with the payment of an enhanced salary. Committees produce hundreds of reports a year on all aspects of government activity, some of them attracting much publicity and helping to lead to significant changes in policy and practice.

With the growth in the welfare state, more and more MPs found themselves providing help and assistance to individual constituents. Rich or influential MPs had often in the past been expected to provide some benefits to those that voted for them, but the scale and type of their involvement with their constituencies changed dramatically after the Second World War. MPs began to set up advice surgeries, enabling large numbers of constituents with specific problems with government bureaucracy, at a national or local level, to ask them to put pressure on departments or councils to address their problems and concerns.

In the 19th and early 20th centuries, most MPs were only part-time politicians. Many had a private income, enabling them to devote their time to parliamentary business; many spent much of their time and energies in other occupations, such as journalism, the law, or business. Nowadays, with the demands of constituents, and the increasing workload of select committees and many other aspects of their work in and out of parliament, few MPs are able to maintain a career outside their political one. A modern system of salary and expenses makes it possible for them to work wholly on their parliamentary functions: however, misuse of the system by a number of MPs (and some peers as well) did a huge amount of damage to the reputation of parliament when it came to light in 2009.

Parties remain key to the organisation of the business and operation of parliament. But MPs tend, now, to be much more independent of their party leaderships than they have been since the late 19th century. Far more of them are speaking or voting from time to time against the line taken by the prime minister or the leader of the opposition. There have been major rebellions by backbenchers against the policies of their own side—most famously in the votes over the Iraq war in 2003. The result of all these developments is sometimes said to have made parliament, both the House of Commons and the House of Lords, less predictable and more lively bodies than they once were.

Some might say that the period in which the House would see debates between Titans of the stamp of Churchill, Enoch Powell, Aneurin (Nye) Bevan, the great Labour firebrand of the immediate post-war years, Michael Foot or David Lloyd George, is over. And, if more lively, parliament nevertheless has had to respond with a growing and powerful sense of scepticism about politicians and disillusion with the political process. It has been visible in the declining public attention given to parliament, with less reporting of its proceedings than was once the case—although radio broadcasting and television broadcasting from 1989 have enabled people to see what goes on in the chamber (not all of which—especially prime minister's question time—they have liked). It has been visible too in the rise of a new political party, UKIP, and in the result of the referendum on Scottish independence on 18 September 2014. Such feelings—which are noticeable in many other countries in Europe—are an enormous challenge to parliament and the political system. It is likely that parliament will need to change to respond to them—as it has changed many times over its centuries-old history.

Illustrations

The History of Parliament

THE HISTORY OF PARLIAMENT

The History of Parliament is a research project creating a comprehensive account of parliamentary politics in England, then Britain, from their origins in the 13th century. Unparalleled in the comprehensiveness of its treatment, the History of Parliament is generally regarded as one of the most ambitious, authoritative and well-researched projects in British history. It consists of detailed studies of elections and electoral politics in each constituency, and of closely researched accounts of the lives of everyone who was elected to parliament in the period, together with surveys drawing out the themes and discoveries of the research and adding information on the operation of parliament as an institution. For more information about the History of Parliament, and to access over 20,000 articles on parliamentarians and constituencies, visit www.historyofparliamentonline.org.

ACKNOWLEDGEMENTS

The History of Parliament would like to thank Professor the Lord Morgan FBA and Professor the Lord Norton of Louth for their assistance in preparing this book.

The History of Parliament is particularly grateful to the Dean and Chapter of Lincoln Cathedral and the Curator's Office at the Palace of Westminster for their help with providing images for the book. The Parliamentary Art Collection is owned jointly by the House of Commons and the House of Lords. It is the national collection illustrating the history of parliament and British politics over the centuries. The House of Commons and House of Lords Works of Art Committees pursue active acquisition policies and, since 1990, have expanded the contemporary collection by promoting the work of living artists. Current priorities include the commissioning of portraits of current and recent eminent parliamentarians; reflecting women's contribution to parliament, both pre and post 1918; and acquiring works of art from around the country that showcase the work of regional artists and documents the landscapes of the UK. To find out more about the collection, visit www.parliament.uk/art.

St James's House

Director
Richard Freed
richard.freed@stjamess.org

Head of Editorial
Stephen Mitchell
stephen.mitchell@stjamess.org

Designer
Anna Danby
anna.danby@stjamess.org

Director of Sales
Richard Golbourne
r.golbourne@stjamess.org

Deputy Editor
John Lewis

Senior Production Manager
Becky Wallace

Production Manager
Stephen Flynn

Client Services Manager
Dhruti Patel

Assistant Designer
Tiziana Lardieri

Picture Editor
James Ide

Subeditor
Hannah Astill

Proofreading
Much Better Text

Regal Press Limited
298 Regents Park Road
London N3 2SZ

020 8371 4000
www.stjamess.org

Index